# LOOK WHAT BUSINESS OWNERS JUST LIKE YOU ARE SAYING ABOUT THIS GEM OF A BOOK.

"This powerful, practical book gives you the key to business success. You learn the most important lessons of all to become wealthy."
—BRIAN TRACY, AUTHOR, "TURBOSTRATEGY"

"Oh Boy! The question isn't whether or not you should buy this book—it's whether you can finish reading it before you get to work tomorrow."
—SETH GODIN, AUTHOR, "PURPLE COW"

"*Never Run Out of Cash* is a must read for anyone involved in business. Philip has written an easy-to-read guide with practical tips and strategies you can implement immediately."
—JILL GRIFFIN, AUTHOR, "CUSTOMER LOYALTY: HOW TO EARN IT, HOW TO KEEP IT"

"This is a revolutionary money-management book. Throw out all the other complicated methods of handling projections and financial strategizing—use Philip's Peace of Mind schedule to get just that—Peace of Mind about your cash flow!"
—DR. JOE VITALE, BEST-SELLING AUTHOR OF "SPIRITUAL MARKETING" AND NUMEROUS OTHER WORKS

"*Never Run Out of Cash* reveals a very simple but very real solution for properly managing your cash flow. You owe it to yourself and your business to read this book—now."
—DEBRA BENTON, AUTHOR, "EXECUTIVE CHARISMA"

"*Never Run Out of Cash* is a must-read and must-use for business owners, operators, and accountants. As a former CFO and a business owner, I know how few people really understand how to project and manage cash.
Philip gets it. And he explains it in a way you can use.
You will learn the important questions. More importantly, you will learn how to answer them so that YOU never run out of cash."
—STEVE KOINIS, ENTREPRENEUR

"Small business lives and dies by one word, Cash-Flow! Many a business owner has seen the finish line of success, only to get blown out of the race by lack of cash . . . the gasoline of everyday business operations.
Philip Campbell's book shows you not only how to manage the dollars and cents of cash-flow, but also how to manage your attitude and beliefs about it . . . something I've never seen anywhere else.

If you want to learn how to finally solve your cash-flow problems—get this book now!"

—JIM EDWARDS, AUTHOR, "IMMEDIATE MONEY IMMEDIATELY"

"I was looking for something just like this. I am also a CPA turned business coach; my focus is on the future not the past, which is not typical for most CPA's. I teach business owners how to get a handle on their cash.

Your book is very easy to understand . . . I will recommend this book to all my clients."

—ALECIA CAINE, CPA, FINANCIAL AND BUSINESS COACH

" *Never Run Out of Cash* has helped me get back to doing what I do best—taking care of customers and growing my business. I never realized how much of my time was wasted worrying about my money. I only wish I had learned the secrets of taking control of my business earlier.

The two questions have made an incredible difference for me. I no longer worry about my cash flow because I can answer the two questions—YES.

I highly recommend that you follow Philip's step-by-step process. It was so easy to do. It made all the difference for me. Now I'm finally back to having fun growing my business."

—RICKY HUX, OWNER AND PRESIDENT, BEST FIT SOLUTIONS, LLC

"Philip, I cannot say thank you enough.

The information in your book is absolutely critical to running any successful business. Without a doubt, failure is certain without the knowledge that you provide. I know, I've been there one too many times!

I owe you a great deal, because I now know how to permanently avoid that 'how did I get here, again?' experience of not having enough cash to continue.

Thank you, thank you, thank you!"

—ANISA AVEN, OWNER, CREATAVISION ENTERPRISES

"This book is GREAT!

Without a degree in accounting, I needed something like Philip's Peace of Mind schedule to keep me focused on the most important aspect of my business—CASH.

It's easy to understand and apply—just what I needed!"

—SYLVIA BARNES, OWNER, LEAP OF FAITH ENTERPRISES

"Philip, absolutely awesome!

Your straightforward advice really struck a chord with me. I have used a similar, albeit incomplete schedule to forecast cash flow for quite some time now. However, your Peace of Mind schedule helped bring into focus some of the areas in my forecasting that needed refining for a more accurate picture.

I think I knew this all along. But there was something about the way you presented it that finally made me do it. I did it immediately after reading the book. Rules # 7 and # 9 are absolutely critical for all business owners and financial managers to live by in order to prosper in business and be able to sleep at night.

Now I'm completely in the driver's seat. My business is so much easier to manage now."
—DAVID SEGERS, CHIEF FINANCIAL OFFICER, WILLIAM COLE, INC.

"This book helps business owners regain control of the financial side of their business, be it an online or an offline business. The message is presented in a very memorable way that is easy to understand and easy to implement."
—WINSTON SCOVILLE, OWNER, MKOPPS SMALL BUSINESS PUBLICATIONS

"Wow, what a wealth of information! I am now much more informed on the subject of cash flow for my own business . . . And much better prepared to answer questions from my clients. You do not charge enough for your book. The information contained in your book, if implemented by every small business, will change the dreadful statistics about the failure rate of those businesses. An excellent piece of work."
—ROBERT J. JACOBS, OWNER, THE CASHXCHANGE GROUP

"Philip's book has completely changed the way I manage my business. I feel that I finally have a clear picture of my financial situation and am now in control. The book was informative, easy for the layman like me to understand and use, above all . . . it works!"
—KATHRYN EDLER, HYPNOTHERAPIST

"There is a lot of talk about cash flow these days, but very little practical instruction on actually knowing how to define it precisely for your business. I think you have gone beyond what was needed and provided an excellent and easy to use tool to assist business owners and managers in steering and growing their companies. I give you two thumbs up on this easy to read business book masterpiece!"
—BILL WHITE, PRESIDENT/CEO, THE BIGGEST DEAL, INC.

# Never
# Run Out
# of
# CASH

# Never
# Run Out
# of
# CASH

---

*The 10 Cash Flow Rules*
*You Can't Afford to Ignore*

---

How to eliminate your cash flow worries
and take control of your business.

Philip Campbell

Grow and Succeed Publishing

Printed in the United States of America

ISBN: 1-932743-00-6

LCCN: 2003113913

Publisher:
Grow and Succeed Publishing, LLC
22211 Buescher Rd.
Tomball, Texas 77377
*www.growandsucceed.com*
*www.neverrunoutofcash.com*

This book is dedicated to my parents who made it possible for me to get my business education and develop a career I truly enjoy.

Thank you for your investment in me.

# Acknowledgments

I'd like to say thank you to some very important people in my life who helped make this book possible and who help me to be a better person each day.

To Wanda Campbell, my beautiful wife and best friend, who is a wonderful mother, a terrific wife, and an all-around warm and friendly person.

To Stephanie Campbell and Daniel Campbell, my daughter and my son, who helped me with several aspects of creating the book and who have shown an incredible amount of kindness and patience with me despite my many shortcomings as a parent.

To all the very bright and hardworking people I have worked with over the years who helped me learn, grow, and succeed in business.

To the group of friends who helped me through all phases of creating this book. Thank you very much for your honest and helpful advice and counsel.

# Send Me Your Questions

I would love to help you experience the success and satisfaction that come from finally taking control of the cash flow of your business.

If you have any questions, concerns, or comments as you read the book, please feel free to send them to me at pcampbell@growandsucceed.com.

I respond to all my e-mail personally and promptly.

I would really enjoy having the opportunity to help you along the way so that you can get the maximum benefit from the material in this book. I want to fulfill my commitment to you and ensure that you have what you need to take control of your cash flow.

If you have any questions while reading a particular chapter or section, you can quickly and easily send me your question by e-mail. I encourage you to use it any time you feel that you need additional information.

I'm here to help you transform the way you manage your business.

Philip Campbell
pcampbell@growandsucceed.com

# Contents

# Introduction

*Without the facts, all we can do is stew around in confusion.*
—DALE CARNEGIE, AUTHOR AND MOTIVATIONAL SPEAKER

My purpose in writing this book is to help make sure you *Never Run Out of Cash.*

As a business owner, you are excited and motivated by the opportunity to create a successful and growing business. You want the opportunity to take control of your financial future and become financially independent. You want the opportunity to achieve the personal fulfillment and satisfaction that comes from doing the work you love and enjoy.

You have invested your time, talent, and financial future in your business in order to enjoy the benefits only a business can deliver. Benefits like:

- The pride of ownership
- More control over your life and how you spend your time
- Not having a boss constantly breathing down your neck
- Making more money
- Creating financial security for yourself and the ones you love

The disturbing trend in business, though, is that the dream of business ownership is too often destroyed by the pain and loss that occur when a business fails. Hundreds of thousands of businesses fail every year. That means hundreds of thousands of people are enduring this very painful and embarrassing process every year.

My experience in business over the last twenty years has convinced me that the single biggest reason the small business failure rates are so incredibly high today is this one simple fact: Most business owners don't really know what's going on with their most precious asset—their CASH.

Despite the fact that cash is the lifeblood of the business, the fuel that keeps the engine running, most business owners don't truly have a handle on the flow of cash into their business and the flow of cash out of their business. As a result, more businesses are failing today than ever before.

I have seen very experienced and seasoned business professionals make incredibly poor business decisions because their focus was on something other than their cash flow. Once they see their business through the lens of its true cash flow, their decisions are oftentimes 180 degrees different. Such a dramatic shift in decision making comes from finally seeing their cash flow in a way that is crystal clear and simple to understand.

In this book, I will share with you a powerful and simple concept that will transform the way you manage your business from this point forward. I will show you how easy it is to take control of your cash flow. I will share with you the principles and the tools that will put you back in control of your business.

At the same time, I will help you discard some of the things you have been taught about managing the financial side of your business that are getting in your way. We will clear away those obstacles so you are perfectly positioned to create the kind of business success you have always dreamed of.

And best of all, you will be in a much better position to avoid the pain and loss associated with failure in business.

You will be amazed at how much easier it is to manage your business properly when you know what's going on with your cash flow. You can grow your business with confidence when you know the cash flow impact of every important business decision you make.

Another objective of this book is:

# To Help You Eliminate Your Cash Flow Worries

Your business will suffer when you get caught up in the negative cycle that begins at the point you start worrying about your cash flow. Your focus begins to shift away from doing what you do best—taking care of customers and making more money.

Questions start to fill your mind such as: "Which vendor are we going to delay payment on? Are we going to be able to make the payroll this week? What are we going to tell the bank? How long is this problem going to last? Is my business going to survive?"

At this point, your focus has shifted away from growing your business, and your energy and enthusiasm begin to wane. At best, this is a recipe for poor performance and mediocrity. At worst, it's a recipe for failure. Yet no one goes into business with the intent to create a mediocre business or to fail.

There is a better way. This book will help you regain control of your business and free you to focus your time and effort on making more money each year.

# Two Crucial Questions

The most important step you can take to eliminate your cash flow worries is to ask yourself two simple questions. These two questions are almost magical in the way they direct your focus to what is most important.

1. What is my cash balance right now?
2. What do I expect my cash balance to be six months from now?

If you can answer each of these questions with a specific number, then you have your cash flow (the lifeblood of your business) under control.

If you cannot answer these questions with a number, then you don't have your cash flow under control. You are not properly managing the most precious asset your business owns.

What happens in your mind when you know that something important in your life and your business is not under control? *Fear.*

And what does fear create in your mind? *Worry.*

Fear is the root cause of worry. Eliminate fear and worry will be eliminated as well. Dale Carnegie, in his wonderful book *How to Stop Worrying and Start Living,* provides excellent advice about how to eliminate fear and worry.

---

1. Get the facts. Without the facts, all we can do is stew around in confusion.
2. Analyze the facts.
3. Arrive at a decision—then act on that decision.

—*Dale Carnegie, How to Stop Worrying and Start Living*

---

With cash flow, having the facts means knowing what your cash balance is right now and knowing what you expect it to be in the near future. When you can answer the two cash flow questions, you have all the facts you need to be in control. You'll be amazed at how having the answers to these two questions will free you from doubt and worry.

Once you know what your cash balance is and what you expect it to be in six months, you can decide whether you like the answers or not.

If you like the answers, great. You then can put all your energy into your plan to make sure the revenue and expenses come in the way you want them to. You are free to focus your time and talents on what you do best—taking care of customers and making more money.

If you don't like the answers, then it is time to create a plan to change the numbers. You have a six-month "heads up" that a problem is looming.

You have a window of opportunity to create a plan and put the plan into action.

## Cash Flow Problems Don't "Just Happen"

I recently used the two questions mentioned previously with our family finances. I had decided to take some time away from my day-to-day business and devote my attention to researching a business idea that I had been considering. About mid-way into my research, I answered the two questions regarding our family finances.

I found that I didn't like the answer to question #2. I looked at the number for what I expected our cash balance to be six months in the future and I didn't like the result.

I took the time to think through what I wanted the cash balance to be. I then considered how I could make that goal a reality. Shortly after, I created a list of three action steps that would get me where I wanted to be in terms of that cash balance.

Over the next three months, I implemented the plan and achieved my objective. My cash balance became what I wanted it to be. That never would have happened if I had not answered question #2 six months before, decided I didn't like the answer, and created a plan to change it.

Think about what the alternative would have been. If I had not seen the problem ahead of time, I would not have known it was a problem until it hit. And that's a terrible time to figure out you have a cash flow problem.

Remember, cash flow problems don't "just happen." They can almost always be seen long before they occur. Your job is to figure out what you expect the cash balance to be six months from now—that way you're in control.

## THE PEACE OF MIND SCHEDULE

The key to answering question #2 is having the right tool. The standard financial statements were not intended to help you manage your cash flow.

The standard financial statements that all businesses use are not adequate for answering this question for several reasons. Financial statements are historical, meaning they're always presenting what happened in the past. Compare them to the rearview mirror in your automobile. The rearview mirror is helpful when you need to see what is behind you. However, when you are driving down the highway, your focus needs to be on what's in front of you. You need to have a good, clear view of what's ahead of you in order to get where you are going safely. Looking in the rearview mirror for more than an occasional glance will soon cause you to crash into something in front of you.

We will talk more about the standard financial statements and why they are not the right tool for answering question #2 later in the book.

I created the Peace of Mind Schedule to give you the clear view you need. It's easy to use, yet powerful in providing you insight into your financial future. Use this schedule every month. I would never attempt to run my business without it.

Part Three is dedicated to helping you put the Peace of Mind Schedule to work. You will be amazed at how this schedule will free you from worrying about your cash flow and help you take control of your business.

# THE 10 CASH FLOW RULES YOU CAN'T AFFORD TO IGNORE

After 20 years of helping business owners understand their cash flow, I have created a set of 10 Cash Flow Rules that will help you take control of the lifeblood of your business—your CASH.

Each chapter is devoted to helping you learn and implement one or more of the 10 Cash Flow Rules. Put these rules to work in your business and you will always be able to answer the two critical cash flow questions.

No more wasted time worrying about what's going on with your cash flow. Instead, you can focus your unique talents and abilities each day on ways to grow your business and make more and more money every year. And that's a recipe for success and wealth creation.

I trust you will enjoy the book and use it to make your business even better and stronger than it is now.

I'm here to help you if you need it.

## Send Me Your Questions

If you have any questions, concerns, or comments, please feel free to send them to me at pcampbell@growandsucceed.com. I respond to all my e-mail personally and promptly.

# PART ONE

## IT'S ALL ABOUT THE CASH

# Chapter 1

## Is Your Cash Flow Under Control?

*We must all suffer from one of two pains: the pain of discipline or the pain of regret. The difference is discipline weighs ounces while regret weighs tons.*
—JIM ROHN, AUTHOR, MOTIVATIONAL SPEAKER

I conducted a cash flow survey to find out the degree to which business owners have their cash flow under control. The survey asked the two critical cash flow questions mentioned in the Introduction plus one additional question.

If you have not already taken the survey, please check it out now. It's fast and easy to complete. Your answers to these questions will tell you whether or not you have your cash flow under control.

Go to www.neverrunoutofcash.com/freetools.htm to take the short Cash Flow Survey.

### AND THE SURVEY SAYS . . .

The following is a summary of what the survey results looked like at the time of this writing (the web page listed above will also allow you to see the full survey results as they exist right now).

The results of the survey were quite interesting. Here is each question together with the responses.

1.  Do You Know What Your Cash Balance is Right Now?

    Yes         75%

    No          25%

2.  Where Is the Best Place to Find Out What Your Cash Balance Is Right Now?

    The bank                    56%

    My accounting system        37%

    Other                       7%

3.  Do You Know What Your Cash Balance Is Expected to Be Six Months from Now?

    Yes         21%

    No          79%

The survey results show that the vast majority of people do not have their cash flow under control. This is the reason why many people feel out of control in their business. That's the bad news.

Bill McGuiness, in his excellent book titled *Cash Rules: Learn and Manage the 7 Cash-Flow Drivers for Your Company's Success*, says this:

---

"Ignorance of cash-flow dynamics kills more companies than fraud, fire, competition, technological obsolescence, or anything else.

There are few circumstances that can't be handled and recovered from if key executives and managers have internalized a cash-flow mindset and integrated it into their management style."

—*Bill McGuiness, Cash Rules: Learn and Manage the 7 Cash-Flow Drivers for Your Company's Success*

---

The good news is that by the time you finish this book, you will know exactly what to do so you can answer the cash flow questions correctly. This will put you back in control of your business.

Let's look at each question in the survey and what it says about whether you have your cash flow under control or not.

- **Survey question #1.** Twenty-five percent of business owners said they do not know what their cash balance is right now. That's a big percentage, considering how important cash is to your business. When you don't know your cash balance, it basically means you are neglecting the books. You are not *"doing today's work today."*

  The good news is this problem is easy to fix. Chapter 5 will show you what to do so you always know what your current cash balance is.

- **Survey question #2.** Fifty-six percent of business owners said the best place to find their cash balance is the bank—this answer means that some of the people who answered question #1 correctly (meaning they said they know what their cash balance is right now) mistakenly believe that the bank is where you get your cash balance.

  The bank balance and the cash balance are two different amounts. Rarely will the two ever be the same. Don't make the mistake of confusing the two. More importantly, don't make the mistake of trying to manage your cash flow using the bank balance. It's a prescription for failure. It's also one reason why so many people are worried about their cash flow and never feel like they have it under control. You *reconcile* your bank balance. You don't *manage* from it.

  Chapter 6 will show you why you should never attempt to manage your cash from the bank balance. It includes an example that will prove to you why attempting to manage from the bank balance leads to mistakes, confusion, and frustration.

- **Survey question #3.** Seventy-nine percent of business owners said they do not know what they expect their cash balance to be six months from now. When you answer this question with "I don't know," then you are headed down a path that could lead to the failure of your business.

  You absolutely, positively cannot run a business and not know what you expect your cash balance to be. Most of the important business decisions you have to make each day cannot be made intelligently without knowing what you expect your cash balance to be over the next six months.

  Most decisions require an outlay of cash at a future date. It's dangerous to make commitments when you are unsure whether you can meet them or not. In addition, you need to have a clear and precise goal for exactly what you want the cash balance to be in the future. That's the only real and lasting measure of financial success in your business.

  I created a schedule that makes it easy to know what your cash balance is expected to be over the next six months. The schedule is called the "Peace of Mind Schedule." The Peace of Mind Schedule has made a huge impact on everyone who has used it.

  The largest portion of this book is devoted to helping you answer that all-important question. When you answer it with a confident *yes,* then you will have put yourself in control of your business.

# Your Action Plan

✔ Take the cash flow survey to see where you stand on the critical cash flow questions. Go to www.neverrunoutofcash.com/freetools.htm to take the survey right now.

✔ Make the commitment to do what it takes to ensure that you can answer each question correctly. You owe it to yourself and to your business.

✔ Commit to learning and using the Peace of Mind Schedule. This schedule will transform the way you manage your business. You will look back at this commitment as an important turning point in the evolution of your business.

## Send Me Your Questions

If you have any questions, concerns, or comments, please feel free to send them to me at pcampbell@growandsucceed.com. I respond to all my e-mail personally and promptly.

# Chapter 2

## How You Can Benefit from Getting Your Cash Flow Under Control

*We cannot become what we need to be by remaining what we are.*
—MAX DE PREE, AUTHOR

The above quotation by Max De Pree is quite true. And the best way to move from where you are now to where you want to be is to get a clear picture in your mind of the benefits you will enjoy as you take control of your cash flow. This is the secret to achieving your goals. Create a clear mental picture of what success in this area will look like and what it will bring to you.

Here are some questions that will help you create that picture of success in your mind.

- How will you benefit from taking control of your cash flow?

- How are you going to use the time and energy you free up for yourself as you begin to eliminate your cash flow worries?

- Do you want the wonderful feeling of finally knowing your cash flow is under control?

- Do you want to eliminate the embarrassment that comes from being forced to dodge vendor and supplier calls about their unpaid invoices?

- Will you spend more time with your best customers?

- Will you spend more time creating and implementing marketing and advertising plans to generate more cash for your business?

The following lists some of the benefits I have personally experienced and seen other business owners experience as a result of taking control of their cash flow.

## Benefits of Having Your Cash Flow Under Control

✔ Increasing the likelihood that your business is a success and that you never run out of cash.

✔ Eliminating the worry associated with not knowing what your cash balance is or what it is expected to be over the next six months. Knowing exactly where you are and where you are going to be, in terms of your cash balance, will instantly eliminate worry, stress, and wasted effort.

✔ Freeing yourself to focus on increasing your revenues and reducing costs. You'll be amazed at what you can accomplish when you're not worrying about what's going on with your cash balance.

✔ Knowing you have accurate financial information to make business decisions. You dramatically increase the quality of your decisions when they are made based on your correct cash balance.

✔ Setting specific goals for what you want the cash balance to be is the first step to achieving what you want from your business. With your cash flow under control, you have the necessary information to set meaningful financial goals.

✔ Seeing cash flow problems before they happen. You have a much better chance of solving cash flow problems when you see them in advance. When you have a six-month "heads up" on the problem, you can map out a plan to fix it and put the plan in action. You have a window of opportunity to solve the problem.

Ask yourself this question again—"What are the benefits I will enjoy as I get my cash flow under control?" Take time now to put some serious thought into this question. Really see in your mind how you and your business will benefit from taking control of your cash flow. This exercise will help you connect the "what you want" with the "why you want it." Get a clear, vivid picture in your mind. See yourself putting the principles in this book to work for you. Visualize your success. This is a powerful method for "locking in" on your target.

Take time now to write down the ways you will benefit from having your cash flow under control. Write down and focus on exactly how you will benefit from putting the principles in this book to work in your business.

Keep this list close by so you can refer to it as you read the remainder of the book.

THIS IS HOW I WILL BENEFIT FROM TAKING CONTROL OF MY CASH FLOW

1._____

_____

2._____

_____

3._____

_____

4._____

_____

# Chapter 3

## The 10 Cash Flow Rules

*It is a simple task to make things complex,*
*but a complex task to make them simple.*
—MEYER'S LAW

I have always enjoyed searching out the principles and rules that create success in business. When I find a method or process that gets results, I like to "peel the onion" to identify the rule or principle behind the success. After 20 years of helping business owners understand their cash flow, I have created a set of 10 rules that will help you take control of the lifeblood of your business—your CASH.

These rules will transform the way you manage your business. You will see your business in a whole new light after you learn these principles and put them into action.

One of the best ways to communicate how helpful these 10 Cash Flow Rules will be for you is to share a wonderful story with you. The author of this story was asked to write a summary of her life. It had to fit on one page and be no more than five chapters long.

Here is how she described the story of her life:

# AUTOBIOGRAPHY IN FIVE SHORT CHAPTERS

## From the book "There Is a Hole in My Sidewalk"

## By Portia Nelson

### Chapter 1

I walk down the street.
There is a deep hole in the sidewalk.
I fall in.
I am lost . . . I am helpless.
It isn't my fault.
It takes me forever to find a way out.

### Chapter 2

I walk down the same street.
There is a deep hole in the sidewalk.
I pretend I don't see it.
I fall in again.
I can't believe I am in the same place
but it isn't my fault.
It still takes a long time to get out.

### Chapter 3

I walk down the same street.
There is a deep hole in the sidewalk.
I see it is there.
I still fall in . . . it's a habit.
My eyes are open.
I know where I am.
It is my fault.
I get out immediately.

> ### *Chapter 4*
> I walk down the same street.
> There is a deep hole in the sidewalk.
> I walk around it.
> ### *Chapter 5*
> I walk down another street.

When you get that feeling that you are not sure what's going on with your cash flow, then you have fallen into your own version of the hole in your sidewalk—the hole that bogs you down and prevents you from using your unique talents and abilities to grow your business and make more money.

The 10 Cash Flow Rules provide you the step-by-step proven process so you can move directly to Chapter 5 in your business life. It's not necessary to keep falling into the same hole with your business. You can use these rules to save yourself an enormous amount of time and energy. Moving directly to Chapter 5 in your business life will simplify your work and make it easier for you to create the kind of business you have always dreamed of.

And if you ever do find yourself in the same hole again, use the 10 Cash Flow Rules to get yourself out. They will provide you the tools and inspiration you need to regain control of your cash flow and put yourself back in the driver's seat. They will transform the way you manage your business from this point forward.

## SUMMARY OF THE 10 CASH FLOW RULES

Each of the following chapters is devoted to helping you learn and implement one or more of the 10 Cash Flow Rules. We will discuss each rule and the step-by-step process for implementing each one.

Before we get to the detailed discussion of each rule, I have provided a brief summary of each one to acquaint you with the tips and strategies we will discuss in more depth throughout the remainder of the book.

### 1. Never Run Out of Cash

Running out of cash is the definition of failure in business. Make the commitment to do what it takes so it does not happen to you.

### 2. Cash Is King

It's important to recognize that cash is what keeps your business alive. Manage it with the care and attention it deserves. It's very unforgiving if you don't. Remember, Cash Is King, because No Cash = No Business.

### 3. Know the Cash Balance Right Now

What is your cash balance right now? It's absolutely critical that you know exactly what your cash balance is. Even the most intelligent and experienced person will fail if he or she is making business decisions using inaccurate or incomplete cash balances. That's the reason business failures are not limited to amateurs or people new to the business world.

### 4. Do Today's Work Today

The key to keeping an accurate cash balance in your accounting system is to do today's work today. When you do this, you will have the numbers you need—when you need them.

### 5. Either You Do the Work or Have Someone Else Do It

Here is a simple rule to follow to make sure you have an accurate cash balance on your books. You do the work or have someone else do it. Those are the only two choices you have. The work must be done. It's like mowing the lawn. You can't just ignore it. Someone has to do it. That means either you do it or you have someone else do it.

### 6. Don't Manage from the Bank Balance

The bank balance and the cash balance are two different animals. Rarely will the two ever be the same. Don't make the mistake of confusing them. It's futile (and frustrating) to attempt to manage your cash flow using the bank balance. It's a prescription for failure. You *reconcile* your bank balance. You don't *manage* from it.

### 7. Know What You Expect the Cash Balance to Be Six Months from Now

What do you expect your cash balance to be six months from now? This one question will transform the way you manage your business. This question really gets to the heart of whether you are managing your business or whether your business is managing you.

### 8. Cash Flow Problems Don't "Just Happen"

You would be shocked and amazed at the number of businesses that fail because the owner did not see a cash flow problem in time to do something about it. The key is to always be able to answer the question— what do I expect my cash balance to be six months from now?

### 9. You Absolutely, Positively Must Have Cash Flow Projections

Cash flow projections are the key to making wise and profitable business decisions. They give you the answer to the all-important question from Rule #7. It's impossible to run your business properly without them.

### 10. Eliminate Your Cash Flow Worries So You Are Free to Do What You Do Best—Take Care of Customers and Make More Money

This is the real key to your success in business. The reason you have to make sure you have the cash flow of your business under control is so you are free to focus all your time and talents where you can make the most difference in your business.

When you have your cash flow under control, you are free from worry, doubt, and concern. You have the cash flow information you need to make sure that everything you do each day in your business is clearly focused on making your business better. You have the information you need to measure your progress using the amount of cash you generate (and keep) for yourself and your business as your ultimate financial measurement.

## LOOK AT THEM EVERY DAY

I have posted the Cash Flow Rules on my web site so you can print them easily. Go to www.neverrunoutofcash.com/freetools.htm and click on the link to get a printer friendly copy of the Cash Flow Rules.

In order to get the most out of these principles, print three copies of the Cash Flow Rules (p. 19). Put one copy on your desk, one copy on your office wall, and one copy on your bathroom mirror (seriously—we will be referring back to this tip a little later in the book).

Looking at this list each day will begin to reinforce these rules in your mind. Soon they will be an important part of your business.

## Send Me Your Questions

If you have any questions, concerns, or comments, please feel free to send them to me at pcampbell@growandsucceed.com. I respond to all my e-mail personally and promptly.

# The 10 Cash Flow Rules

1. Never Run Out of Cash.

2. Cash Is King.

3. Know the Cash Balance Right Now.

4. Do Today's Work Today.

5. Either You Do the Work or Have Someone Else Do It.

6. Don't Manage from the Bank Balance.

7. Know What You Expect the Cash Balance to Be Six Months from Now.

8. Cash Flow Problems Can Be Seen in Advance.

9. You Absolutely, Positively Must Have Cash Flow Projections.

10. Eliminate Your Cash Flow Worries So You Are Free to Do What You Do Best—Grow Your Business and Make More Money.

# Chapter 4

## Cash Is King

*Cash Is King, because No Cash = No Business.*

One of the cold, hard realities of business is that if you ever run out of cash, your business is finished. All your hard work goes right down the drain. Your dreams and desires for creating an exciting and profitable business come crashing down. As one of my favorite authors, Brian Tracy, says: "This Is Not for You!"

The statistics on small business failures are alarming. Michael Gerber, author of *The E-Myth: Why Most Small Businesses Don't Work and What to Do About It*, says this:

> "Businesses start and fail in the United States at an increasingly staggering rate. Every year, over a million people in this country start a business of some sort. Statistics tell us that by the end of the first year at least 40 percent of them will be out of business.
>
> Within five years, more than 80 percent of them will have failed.
>
> And the rest of the bad news is, if you own a small business that has managed to survive for five years or more, don't breathe a sigh of

> relief. Because more than 80 percent of the small businesses that survive the first five years fail in the second five."
>
> —*Michael Gerber, The E-Myth Revisited*

Wow! Those statistics are incredible—and scary. Just think: For every five businesses started, four of them will fail within five years. Only one of the five will be left standing.

Which category will you be in? And why does a business fail? There are a number of contributing factors; however, they can all be summed up like this:

## THEY RAN OUT OF CASH

What I find fascinating about these statistics is what's hidden beneath the data. Is running out of cash just one of those things a vast majority of businesses should expect?

Seth Godin and Paul Lim, authors of *If You're Clueless About Accounting and Finance and Want to Know More* said this:

> "At the very least, your company must ensure at all times it has enough cash in its accounts to meet short-term obligations as they come due.
>
> After all, business can make the most innovative products and reduce expense through the most innovative management techniques.
>
> But if it doesn't have enough money to pay its bills, all these efforts will be for naught."
>
> —*Seth Godin and Paul Lim, If You're Clueless About Accounting and Finance and Want to Know More*

Is every business destined to struggle to generate enough cash to pay all the bills *and* pay you a generous return? How many of these businesses were profitable but made the mistake of thinking profits were the same as cash?

Here is how the cycle usually works.

- **Cash starts to get tight.** When cash runs low, you get pulled into decisions such as: Which vendor are we going to delay payment on? How will we make the payroll? Are there any expenses we can cut immediately? What are we going to tell the bank?

- **Worry sets in.** Not being able to pay your bills on time is a terrible feeling. You feel like a failure. Your mind runs wild. You start thinking of all the bad things that might happen if your business collapses. It is scary and uncomfortable.

   You are unsure about how long the cash flow problem may last. You don't have a clear sense of whether it's about to get better or it's about to get worse. You don't have a clear view of the extent or duration of the problem.

   It's like riding along on the freeway in a driving rainstorm and you discover that your windshield wipers won't work. You cannot see the cars in front of you or behind you, so you slow down to a crawl. You're just hoping and praying the rain stops before you end up in a terrible accident.

- **Your focus has shifted.** Now you are spending most of your time trying to put out the cash flow fire. You cannot focus on doing what you do best—taking care of customers and making more money. You are now the chief firefighter.

   It is more difficult now to be out working with customers. It's harder to coach and train your people. Even when you do get out there, your mind is still occupied with thoughts about the cash flow fire raging back at the office. The time you spend with your customers and your people is far less productive.

Calls about invoices and payments that would normally go to your bookkeeper or your accounting department are now going to you. Vendors are calling, angry and frustrated, because they are not getting paid on time, if at all. They want answers—from *you.*

The vendors are also questioning whether you will make it or not. They have seen other companies go down the same path. They have seen the failure cycle before. They start asking you what's going on in your business: "Are you going to make it? When can you pay what you owe me?"

- **Your business fails.** When the cycle above sets in, it is very difficult to reverse. As it progresses, it picks up speed, diverts you away from what you do best, and eventually you crash into the proverbial brick wall (going really fast).

Your worst nightmare unfolds. The pain and suffering of failure becomes a day-to-day reality.

It doesn't have to be that way. There is a solution. And it's easier than you may think.

---

### The 10 Cash Flow Rules

*Rule #1*
## Never Run Out of Cash

*Rule #2*
## Cash Is King

---

# Your Action Plan

✔ Never run out of cash.

✔ Resolve now that you will not be one of the 80 percent of businesses that fail in their first five years. Take control of your cash so you are free to focus your talents on growing your business and making more money.

✔ Recognize that cash is what keeps your business alive. Manage it with the care and attention it deserves. It is quite unforgiving if you don't.

## Send Me Your Questions

If you have any questions, concerns, or comments, please feel free to send them to me at pcampbell@growandsucceed.com. I respond to all my e-mail personally and promptly.

# PART TWO

## KNOW THE CASH BALANCE

# Chapter 5

## What Is the Cash Balance Right Now?

*It's all about the CASH.*

What is your cash balance right now?

It's absolutely critical that you know what your current cash balance is. You should be able to put your hands on this number whenever you need it. By that I mean you should know your cash balance within two minutes of needing it. When you can do that, you have this component of your cash flow process under control.

### KEEP AN ACCURATE CASH BALANCE

You have to have an accurate cash balance on your books in order to manage the business intelligently. The balance must be accurate to ensure you are making good financial decisions each day.

Business failures are not just confined to amateurs or people new to the business world. Even the most intelligent and experienced person will fail if he or she is making business decisions using inaccurate or incomplete cash balance information.

Decisions that might otherwise be brilliant become deadly when they are based on inaccurate data. For instance, if you go to the doctor and he or she makes an inaccurate diagnosis, the prescription or treatment you receive could be harmful—even fatal. The diagnosis must be accurate before the proper treatment can be prescribed.

In business, you have to have good numbers, and the most important number of all is the cash balance. You need to know exactly where you stand financially before making important business decisions.

Let's look at what is required to maintain an accurate cash balance in your accounting system.

**Cash Receipts.** Enter the cash receipts shortly after the end of each day. As you receive money in the mail, from credit card sales, and so on, you need to record those transactions in the accounting system. Regardless of whether you made a deposit at the bank that day or not, you still need to post the deposits to your books. (Of course, holding deposits and not bringing them to the bank every day is a bad idea.)

The point here is that even if something happens to prevent the deposit from being physically taken to the bank, you still need to record the transaction in your accounting system. Date and record the transactions in the system on the day you receive the money.

**Vendor Invoices.** There are two important points I'd like to make here. First, enter invoices from your vendors promptly upon receiving them. Don't let them sit around because you don't intend to pay them right away. Get them in the system ASAP.

Second, pay your bills on or before the date they are due. Don't buy into the belief that you are being smart with your money by delaying payment until after the due date. Develop a reputation with your vendors for paying them on time. The outstanding reputation you develop with your vendors is worth ten times more than any interest you may earn by paying your bills late.

Let's go back to the point about entering vendor invoices quickly. One reason for getting the bills in the system quickly is that it gives you an accurate accounts payable balance in your accounting system.

Accounts payable is the dollar amount of bills that have not yet been paid. It's money that is soon to be deducted from your cash balance. This number plays an important role in answering question #2. We will talk more about this question in Part Three.

I have seen many businesses that take way too long to get the invoices in the accounting system. Sometimes the delay is just procrastination. Sometimes it's because the invoices are being routed to several people for approval to pay.

Your standard should be to have invoices entered in the system within a day or two of receiving the invoice. This will ensure your accounts payable are accurate and make it easier to get the bills paid on or before the due date.

**Reconcile the cash balance.** The cash balance needs to be reconciled to the bank balance each month. Every month you receive a bank statement from the bank. The statement shows the beginning bank balance, all the deposits, checks, and other transactions that have cleared the bank, and your ending bank balance.

Reconcile the cash balance to the bank balance promptly. This is not a task to be neglected. It's the perfect way to verify that the cash balance on your books is accurate.

It's also the way you verify that the bank has not made any mistakes with your account.

You have entrusted the bank with a precious asset—your cash. You have to make sure they are caring for your cash accurately. Reconciling the two balances each month is the way you do that.

My recommendation is to have the reconciliation complete within two to three days of receiving the statement from the bank. You will find any problems or errors quickly, which means you can correct them quickly.

# Do Today's Work Today

The key to keeping an accurate cash balance in your accounting system is to do today's work today. When you do, you will have the numbers you need when you need them. You will also be confident the balance is accurate.

Problems occur when you, or the person you have in charge of your books, violates this rule. The trouble begins when entering cash receipts is put off or entering invoices is delayed. "We don't need to enter them today because we won't be paying them for another week or two anyway."

Perhaps you or your spouse has the job of keeping the books. You're busy running the business, taking care of customers, and making the sale. "It's a hassle. It's not as important or as urgent as the hundreds of other responsibilities I have."

So the "data entry" stacks up. It goes in the stack I call the "I know I need to do it, but I can't do it right now" stack. Maybe it gets done once a month. Maybe it takes even longer than that.

To quote Brian Tracy again: "This Is Not for You!"

# Doing the "Dishes" Each Day

Compare your financial recordkeeping to doing the dishes at home. Do you (or someone in your family) do the dishes every day or do you let them pile up for days or weeks until you "get around to it"?

If you've gotten into the habit of putting off the accounting and data entry work, I'd like to suggest a test.

Try this test at home for one full week and see what happens. Here's the test:

**Stop doing the dishes.**

Allow them to stack up for a full week. Save yourself the time and trouble of cleaning up after meals. After you enjoy a good meal, put the dishes in the sink or on the counter and move on to the other important things around the house. Just think how much free time you will create for yourself.

Life is good, right?

Well, maybe not. After the first day or so, a couple of thoughts start to go through your head. "I'm still going to have to do the dishes. When I do, there is going to be a huge stack and it's going to take a long time. After a week, they are also going to be smelly and have old, hardened food all over them."

You would be embarrassed when friends come over and see a dirty pile of dishes stacked up in your kitchen. Then after a week, isn't it a much harder chore?

Ask yourself this question: Do most people do the dishes every day because they just love doing the dishes? Of course not. They do them each day because it's one of those chores that can be overwhelming if neglected for too long. Doing the dishes every day is the practice of doing today's work today. You do it because the alternative approach is a really bad idea.

When you take today's work and save it until tomorrow, all you have done is piled it on to tomorrow's work. You have procrastinated on the false assumption that it will somehow be easier tomorrow.

Doing today's work today is the approach to use in your business. Specifically, make sure the books are kept current each day. This will ensure you have an accurate cash balance.

## EITHER YOU DO THE WORK OR HAVE SOMEONE ELSE DO IT

Here is a simple rule to follow to make sure today's work gets done today.

1. You do the work

   or

2. You have someone else do the work

Those are the only two choices you have. Doing today's work today is a more intelligent approach than piling today's work on top of tomorrow's work. The work must be done. Someone has to do it. That means either you do it or you have someone else do it.

Your job as a business owner or manager involves setting the performance standards, then seeing to it that the job gets done in accordance with the standards you set. You decide if you will be doing the work or if you will have someone else, such as a bookkeeper or accountant, do it. Even if you have a chief financial officer and a full finance and accounting department, the principle still applies. If you have someone else do it, communicate the performance standards, then make sure it gets done.

You must have an accurate cash balance.

---

**The 10 Cash Flow Rules**

*Rule #3*
## Know the Cash Balance Right Now

*Rule #4*
## Do Today's Work Today

*Rule #5*
## Either You Do the Work or Have Someone Else Do It

---

## Your Action Plan

✔ Make a personal commitment that your books and your cash balance will be managed properly every day. You should be able to put your hands on the cash balance within two minutes of needing it.

✔ Make sure the cash balance is accurate. This is about "doing the dishes" every day.

✔ Do today's work today.

✔ Determine whether you will be doing the work or whether someone else will. If it's someone else, communicate clearly what you expect and when you expect it. Then see to it that the job is done in accordance with your standards.

## Send Me Your Questions

If you have any questions, concerns, or comments, please feel free to send them to me at pcampbell@growandsucceed.com. I respond to all my e-mail personally and promptly.

# Chapter 6

## Don't Manage from the Bank Balance

*Efficiency is doing things right; effectiveness is doing the right things.*
—PETER F. DRUCKER, AUTHOR

Fifty-six percent of the small business owners in the cash flow survey said the best place to find out what their cash balance is right now is to get the balance from the bank. How did **YOU** answer this question?

What's the correct answer to the best place to get your cash balance? Your accounting system, not the bank! The bank balance and the cash balance are two different amounts. Rarely will the two ever be the same. Don't make the mistake of confusing the two.

Repeat after me—My bank balance is not my cash balance; my bank balance is not my cash balance; my bank balance is not my cash balance.

It's true that the bank will provide you a balance. If you have online banking, you could even get that balance within the two-minute requirement I recommend.

However, don't make the mistake of trying to manage your cash flow using the bank balance. It's a prescription for failure. You reconcile your bank balance; you don't manage from it.

So what's the problem, you ask? The problem is the bank does not provide you with an accurate cash balance. The bank tells you how much money is in your account *at the bank* at any point in time. Your accounting system tells you what your true cash balance is.

The following example will highlight the difference. Suppose you call the bank or go online to get the bank balance. The bank says you have $10,000 in your account. What business decisions can you now make about the amount of money you have available to you? How can you use the information you just received from the bank to make important business decisions? Can you go to the bank and withdraw the $10,000?

Let's say you just received an invoice today for $9,000. The vendor says you can deduct a 2 percent discount ($180) if you pay within five days. Can you write the check today? Should you write the check now and save $180?

The problem is you don't have enough information to answer these questions. You don't have your true cash balance yet. You are virtually guaranteed of making a bad decision if you use the bank balance to answer these questions.

This is an extremely important point. It's essential that you recognize clearly that you cannot, and absolutely must not, answer these questions based on your bank balance.

## What's the Problem?

Most businesses cut checks and pay their bills every week. How many of the checks you have written over the last few weeks have cleared the bank and been deducted from the bank balance? How many have *not* cleared yet? What's the dollar value of those that have not cleared yet?

Suppose you wrote a check for $8,000 three days ago. Has it cleared yet? Has it been deducted from the $10,000 balance you just got from the bank? If it hasn't cleared yet, then an $8,000 check is on its way to the bank and will be deducted from your bank balance. When it gets there, your balance will go from $10,000 to $2,000.

Look at the impact this has on the questions you just asked yourself. Can you go to the bank and withdraw $10,000? Can you write a check today for $9,000 to pay an invoice you just received? Knowing there is an $8,000 check about to be deducted from your bank balance changes everything. Now you know you cannot withdraw the $10,000 or write a check for $9,000. You can answer these questions now because you have a more accurate view of your real cash balance.

## YOUR ACCOUNTING SYSTEM IS WHERE YOU FIND YOUR CASH BALANCE

Your accounting system records all your cash receipts and disbursements. The accounting system is where the "books" of your company are maintained. This is your bible. This is where your cash balance is maintained.

The difference between your cash balance and your bank balance is primarily a result of the difference in the timing of recording a transaction in your books and the same transaction being recorded (or clearing) at the bank. These differences are "timing differences."

Here is an example.

When you print a check from your accounting system, it is immediately deducted from your cash balance. As the check is sitting on the printer, it has been deducted from the cash balance on your books, even before you have put it in an envelope to mail it.

Has it been deducted from your bank balance yet? No.

The check will not be deducted from your bank balance until it is presented to the bank to be paid. You mail it to your vendor, they receive it and deposit it in their bank, the banking system routes it to your bank, and it is finally paid by your bank. *Now* the check is deducted from your bank balance. The timing difference with the checks you cut represents the time between deducting it on your books and the time it takes to be deducted from your bank account.

The same concept works with cash receipts. When you receive payment from a customer, you fill out the deposit slip, record the deposit on your books, and take the deposit to the bank. In this case, the bank will usually credit your account the next day.

## SAVE YOURSELF TIME AND TROUBLE

Don't try to manage from the bank balance. It is an activity that will only create mistakes, confusion, and frustration.

Use the cash balance on your books to manage your business. Then reconcile that amount to the bank statement each month to make sure both balances are accurate.

You will save yourself a great deal of time and trouble by following this approach.

---

### The 10 Cash Flow Rules

*Rule #6*
## Don't Manage from the Bank Balance

---

# Your Action Plan

✔ Don't manage from the bank balance. You reconcile the bank balance, not manage from it.

✔ Take the time to learn and understand the "timing differences" that make the cash balance and the bank balance different at any given point in time.

✔ Make sure the cash balance is reconciled to the bank balance every month. This ensures that your cash balance is accurate.

## Send Me Your Questions

If you have any questions, concerns, or comments, please feel free to send them to me at pcampbell@growandsucceed.com. I respond to all my e-mail personally and promptly.

# PART THREE

## YOU ABSOLUTELY, POSITIVELY MUST HAVE CASH FLOW PROJECTIONS

# Chapter 7

## What Do You Expect the Cash Balance to Be Six Months from Now?

*The punch that knocks you out is the one you didn't see.*
—JOE FRAZIER, FORMER BOXING CHAMPION

What do you expect your cash balance to be six months from now? This one question will transform the way you manage your business.

The question really gets to the heart of whether you are managing your business or whether your business is managing you. And there is a huge difference between the two.

When you know the answer to this question, you can rest assured you are in control of your cash flow. You are free to focus on what you do best—growing your business and making more money.

When you answer this question with "I don't know," then you are headed down a path that could lead to the failure of your business. You absolutely, positively cannot run a business and not know what you expect the cash balance to be. You will end up wasting your valuable time worrying about what may or may not happen. You need to know what your balance is now and what you expect it to be six months from now—period.

Look at the cash flow survey results in Chapter 1. Seventy-nine percent of the people said they do not know what they expect their cash balance to be in six months. It's the answer to this question that motivated me to write this book. It made me realize how big a problem this is for most people in business. I am excited to be able to help you recognize the problem and create a lasting and simple solution to it.

I encourage you to not only read this chapter, but also to commit to take the steps I set out for you. Solving this problem will have a dramatic, positive impact on your business and your life the same way it has for me.

Let's get to it.

## BENEFITS OF KNOWING YOUR FUTURE CASH FLOW

There are several important benefits you will realize from knowing what you expect your cash balance to be six months from now.

- You will have a goal set for the most important measurement of success in business. Most people have not set specific goals for what they want their cash balance to be. As a result, too many people fail to achieve the level of financial success they deserve.

- You will see possible cash flow problems long before they happen. You can then control what actually *does* happen.

- You can create a plan to get your cash balance where you want it to be.

- You will have the peace of mind that comes from knowing your cash flow is under control. This will free your mind from worrying about cash flow so you can focus on what you do best—taking care of customers and making more money.

Let's discuss these benefits in more detail.

**Having Cash Balance Goals.** Your goal is to make money. Money is cash. If you are not generating cash in your business, then you are not achieving the objective. You can quantify what you define financial success to be by putting a dollar value on the amount of cash you want to generate from your business.

Profits can't be spent. Only cash can be spent. The measure of your success in business will be determined by how much cash you create and how much of that cash you hang on to. Therefore, you must have a goal for exactly what you want your cash balance to be.

A goal will solidify in your mind exactly what you need the business to do for you financially. Your focus on cash will have an amazing impact on your ability to create a business that takes care of you financially.

**Seeing Problems Before They Happen.** Knowing what your cash balance is expected to be in six months gives you tremendous power, not to mention giving you the peace of mind of knowing that you are in control of your business—and your cash balance.

You can finally get the cash flow "monkey" off your back.

Seeing possible problems well before they can become a reality gives you visibility into the future. This is a huge benefit. It's hard to overstate just how important this is in everything you do.

To know what your cash balance is expected to be six months from now means you have monthly cash flow projections for at least the next six months. We will talk more in the coming chapters about a simple but incredibly powerful tool for creating and maintaining your projections. This is a schedule you *cannot* run your business without.

Joe Frazier said this:

> "The punch that knocks you out is the one you didn't see."
>
> —*Joe Frazier*

What Joe Frazier was saying is that in boxing, if you see the punch coming, you have a chance to react. You have time to get out of the way—you can at least "roll with the punch." It's when you don't see the punch coming that you get knocked out.

In business, if you do not see a cash flow problem coming, then you will not be prepared when the problem arrives on your doorstep. Most people don't have a good idea of what their cash balance is going to be until it becomes a crisis. That's how businesses are ruined.

Even if you believe you will have a cash shortage in the future, you still need to see it in advance. You must recognize the shortage, calculate how much it might be, and predict precisely when it is likely to happen.

You must understand and define the possible implications on your business.

You have the time between now and then to adjust and "roll with the punch." You can plan for it by making changes in other areas. If you plan for the punch in advance, you can avoid it before it lands on the side of your head.

You do not want the punch to show up at the last minute, when you do not see it coming. This kind of surprise blow will knock you out. It could be the kind of blow that ruins your business.

**Creating a Plan and Putting it to Work.** If you see a problem coming, you can create a specific list of steps to try to fix it. Once you have a precise estimate of the dollar amount of the problem, you will know how big or small the problem may be.

To know you have a possible cash flow problem is not enough information to get you to a solution. That sentence bears repeating one more time.

To know you have a possible cash flow problem is not enough information to get you to a solution.

You have to know how much of a problem you have and *when* it will be a problem. You have to put a dollar amount and a time-frame on the problem.

For example, which of the following statements will help move you to a solution?

1. I'm concerned I may be short of cash sometime soon!
   or
2. I expect to be $5,000 short of cash at the end of April.

Neither statement is good news. However, the second statement gives you the information you need to do something about the problem. You know how much you expect the problem to be and when it is likely to become a reality. Now you can make a list of all the ways you can increase revenues, reduce expenses, reduce capital expenditures, restructure debt obligations, and so on.

This helps you focus on creating a specific plan so you can take action. The key to success in business is to have a clear goal in mind, create a specific plan to achieve the goal, implement the plan, then measure your progress against the plan. You can dramatically increase the likelihood that you and your business are a huge financial success.

You are now focusing your unique talents, abilities, and drive toward growing the business and making more money every year. This is an effective strategy that will greatly increase your chances of success. Use it properly and your business will grow and prosper. And that's the objective, right?

**Having Peace of Mind and Freedom from Worry.** Knowing what your cash balance is expected to be six months from now means you have the cash flow process under control. This frees your mind in an important and interesting way.

When your mind is thinking, "I don't know if I can pay the bills tomorrow," or "I don't know if I will be able to meet the payroll next Friday," then fear and panic begin to set in.

You may be in a sales presentation with your most important customer and your mind will drift back to the problem. "How am I going to deliver on my promise to this customer when I don't even know if I will be in business in two months. If he talks to my vendors, will he find out we can't pay our bills on time?"

Your ability to focus on fixing the problem is severely minimized. Worry and concern will drain you of energy and divert your mind from getting things done.

It's like pouring sand in your car's engine. Bad things happen. The faster you try to go, the more damage you do to the engine. Your productivity and effectiveness come to a grinding halt.

On the other hand, when you know what the cash balance is expected to be, your mind is free from worry and concern. You have a clear view of what is coming. You can act with confidence to implement your business plan knowing where you are going and how you will get there.

---

## The 10 Cash Flow Rules

### *Rule #7*
### Know What You Expect the Cash Balance to Be Six Months from Now

---

## Your Action Plan

✔ Knowing what you expect your cash balance to be six months from now will transform the way you manage your business. Commit now to put this principle to work in your business.

✔ You can solve cash flow problems when you see them in advance. When you have a six-month "heads up" on the problem, you can map out a plan to fix the problem and put the plan in action. You have six months to solve the problem.

✔ Having a clear view of what is likely to happen frees your mind from worry. Not knowing what the cash balance is expected to be is what creates worry.

✔ When you eliminate your cash flow worries, you can focus 100 percent of your unique talents and abilities on growing your business and making more money.

## Send Me Your Questions

If you have any questions, concerns, or comments, please feel free to send them to me at pcampbell@growandsucceed.com. I respond to all my e-mail personally and promptly.

# Chapter 8

## Cash Flow Problems Don't "Just Happen"

*One of the primary reasons for worry and concern over difficulties is contained in the failure to define it clearly in the first place.*
—BRIAN TRACY, AUTHOR, MANAGEMENT EXPERT

You would be shocked and amazed at the number of businesses that fail because the owner did not see a cash flow problem in time to do something about it. One thing I want to really help you to see is that cash flow problems can almost always be seen far enough in advance to do something about it.

It is a myth to think that cash flow problems "just happen." Rarely is a cash flow problem a sudden event. It is almost always something that accumulates over a period of time, and it is not difficult to see it coming.

Here is a real life example I experienced while working with a small business.

The president of the company had some concerns about his accounts receivable. He thought the process for collecting receivables from his customers was not functioning as well as it could. Money was tight and he believed the primary reason was a slow-down in collecting receivables from his customers.

The first thing I did was to ask the two critical questions from this book:

1. What is the cash balance right now?
2. What do you expect the cash balance to be six months from now?

He didn't know the answers. His response was that cash was "a little tight right now." This turned out to be a dramatic understatement.

My next step was to spend some time in the accounting department, which, as the keepers of the accounting records, is where one should be able to find the answers to the questions. And find the answers I did!

Here is what I found:

- Cash wasn't just "a little tight right now." The dollar amount of vendor invoices in the system to be paid (accounts payable) was three times more than the cash available to pay the invoices. More than half of the invoices were already past due.

- Not all the invoices had been entered in the accounting system. There were fairly recent invoices that were sitting in a stack to be entered later. The accounting department personnel were in no rush to enter the invoices because they knew they would not be able to pay them anytime soon.

    The reports that had been printed to show the cash balance and the accounts payable balance (bills to be paid from the cash balance) did not even show these bills.

    These invoices went into a stack I call the "these will be entered closer to when they can actually be paid" stack. I have seen this happen in many companies that have cash flow problems. Accounting is forced to delay payment on some invoices and not pay others at all. Vendors then start calling to demand their money.

The vendor's favorite question is, "When will I get paid?" After several calls, they start to sense that the company is in trouble. Then they get upset and rude with the person on the phone. That's when it gets ugly—and a bit personal.

It's hard for the clerk in accounting to take the heat from a vendor who feels like he is being cheated by the company. The vendor provided a product or service to the company and he wants his money when it was promised. The vicious cycle continues.

Accounting is now spending much more of its time fending off vendor calls. Another chunk of time is spent fending off people inside the company who are also irritated because vendors are starting to call them and threatening to cut off products or services.

- A small amount of cash was on hand but had been put off limits for paying the bills. Accounting had been instructed not to use that cash because it was to be used for an investment that was planned in about 30 days.

- A schedule had been prepared that attempted to project cash flows for the next 12 months. However, the approach to the schedule was confusing (for the business people and the accountants) and difficult to understand.

(Note: Part Three of this book will show you the proper way to project cash flows and cash balances that is both simple to prepare and easy to understand.)

## THE DECISIONS CAME EASY ONCE THE FACTS WERE CLEAR

I reported back to the president what I had found. My approach when I do this for a business is to bring them the answers to the two key cash flow questions. My job is to make sure they can answer the two questions instantly from the information I provide.

In this case, I sat down with the president and gave him the facts and a list of what needed to be done. We reviewed the findings and precisely what was going on with his cash balance.

Here is a summary of the realizations he came to after seeing the cash flow information in a new way:

1. His books were not accurate. All the invoices from vendors were not yet in the accounting system. Any numbers he looked at from the system right now were inaccurate. He realized this was a big problem that had to be fixed immediately. He had bad financial information.

2. He had to abandon the planned investment. He now could see clearly that if he made this investment, the company would run out of cash within three to six months of writing the check.

3. The cash set aside for the investment should be used to pay all existing vendor invoices. He realized that he could not run a company that does not pay its bills. It was an incredible waste of time for him (and all the other people in the company who were constantly fighting the cash flow fire) and it was a terrible business practice. The president was being forced to divert his focus from doing what he did best—taking care of customers and selling more product.

4. His accounts receivable collections had slowed somewhat, but not as much as he thought they had. He realized this was only a small part of the cash flow problem.

The president was genuinely surprised at the size of his cash flow problem. He knew the cash balance was uncomfortably low, and he knew "some bills" were not being paid on time. What he didn't know was that the past due bills dwarfed his cash balance. He also did not realize there was a stack of invoices that had not even been entered in the accounting system yet. The reports he was being provided from time to time about the cash and unpaid bill problems were not accurate. They were incomplete.

As a result, if he had continued along the path he was on, he would have written the check to make the investment that had previously been planned. He would have done it on the assumption that the company could continue managing with cash being "a little tight right now."

## THE TWO CRITICAL CASH FLOW QUESTIONS SAVED THE COMPANY

Once the president knew the answers to the two critical cash flow questions, he knew he had to change course—and do it fast.

Presented with the answer to what he expected the cash balance to be six months from now, he knew exactly what he had to do.

The president knew that the investment could not be made.

It became perfectly clear that making the investment would bankrupt the company within just a few months of making it, all because he did not have an accurate view of what the company's cash balance was expected to be in six months.

This was an important realization for him and his business.

Before he had the answers to the two questions, he felt confident in making the decision to go forward with the investment. After he had the answers to the two questions, he was confident in making the decision *not* to go forward with the investment.

The exact opposite decision was made once he had an accurate view of his cash balance and where it was expected to be over the next six months. This made all the difference for his company.

Have you ever tried to make an important decision like this without knowing the facts? Don't make this mistake in your business.

The Peace of Mind Schedule will give you the information you need to make intelligent and effective business decisions.

---

**The 10 Cash Flow Rules**

*Rule #8*
Cash Flow Problems Can Be Seen in Advance

---

# Your Action Plan

✔ Cash flow problems can almost always be seen far in advance of their actually happening. Make a commitment to invest the time necessary to be able to answer the question, "What do I expect the cash balance to be six months from now?"

✔ Never be caught by surprise. It's like trying to drive down the freeway with your windshield covered in mud. Take the time to wash the mud off so you have a clear view of what is in front of you. It reduces the chance of accidents tremendously.

✔ Make business decisions with a view to the impact they have on your future cash flow. This will greatly improve your ability to make prudent and profitable decisions.

✔ Rarely is a cash flow problem a sudden event. Be smart about managing your cash flow and your business.

# Send Me Your Questions

If you have any questions, concerns, or comments, please feel free to send them to me at pcampbell@growandsucceed.com. I respond to all my e-mail personally and promptly.

# Chapter 9

## The Peace of Mind Schedule Is Born

*Necessity is the Mother of Invention.*

It was a beautiful, warm evening in 1994. The CEO and I had just signed the papers on a deal that generated a profit of $3.5 million for our company. It was the most money the company had ever made.

We sat on the patio of the restaurant to toast the occasion. We were thrilled to have finally closed the deal. We felt so proud to have closed a deal that made so much money for the company. We also felt a sense of relief that it was finally done.

After our toast, we reflected on the four years that led up to this huge profit.

One thing was certain: there was a time in the early days of the company when we didn't think things were going to work out at all.

I would like to share with you the story of how the Peace of Mind Schedule came into existence.

The events that occurred during this four-year period made a big difference in my career and taught me the proper way to manage the cash flow of a business.

I will share with you how this schedule helped our company get through an extremely difficult cash flow crunch and create the most profitable deal in our company's history.

## Is Our Cash Problem Going to Get Worse?

Four years before, we had bought a division of a public company. Cash was tight from day one. The deal was financed with a good bit of debt, a large portion of which was scheduled to be paid off within the first two years.

I was still new to the role of being the financial officer inside a company. I had spent the previous seven years working in CPA firms. The first three-and-a-half years I worked for a local public accounting firm. The next three-and-a-half years I spent with one of the large international accounting firms.

Being new to my financial duties, I found myself a bit uneasy with the cash management process in general. I had a budget, but that didn't really help much when it came down to figuring out which bills we could pay. It also didn't help when I tried to figure out if our cash flow problems were temporary or not.

I relied primarily on the budget and the income statement as my guide. It never got so bad that I was forced to use a different tool. But I knew in that first year that I was flying blind with regard to cash flow. I knew I didn't really have the cash flow under control.

The nagging question that was always in the back of my mind was, "Is this problem going to get worse?" We were forced to pay vendor invoices late. We had rescheduled some of our debt obligations with our primary lender in order to avoid defaulting on the debt.

After the first year, the cash flow problem got worse. Sales were off a bit and more of the debt was scheduled to be paid off. We were routinely holding invoices from vendors and the invoices we *were* paying were being paid late. I could see that the next payment due on the debt could not be paid. That was the big wake-up call.

# LATE PAYMENTS BRING IMPATIENCE

While our lender had been working with us through our cash flow problems, they were becoming impatient. Worse, they were beginning to question whether the management team really had the cash flow of the business under control. We needed new payment terms and a new payment structure so we could pay the debt and not have to keep going back to them with excuses about how we were unable to meet our commitments.

That's the point where I said, "Not only do I need something better for me and for the rest of our management team, I need something to help me clearly show our lender what's going on financially." At this point, I was getting tired of failing to meet our financial commitments and worrying about whether we had a handle on our cash flow.

It was clear to me we needed to do something quick. We had to renegotiate the terms of the debt with our lender or we would default on the loan. And default could mean the end of the company. I summarized what needed to be accomplished as follows:

- I needed a schedule that would help me figure out exactly what we could afford to pay on the debt. I knew we could not afford to pay the debt as it currently was coming due but I didn't know exactly what we could afford.

- I needed a way to present a clear and easy-to-understand picture of the financial situation we were in to the lender. I thought that if they had a clear view of our finances, they would be more likely to go along with our plan.

- The financial picture needed to show clearly how the cash flow of the company tied into the income statement. Specifically, it needed to show how the cash flow compared to the primary financial measure we used to track performance. Our Earnings

Before Interest, Taxes, Depreciation and Amortization (EBITDA) was the primary performance measure we used internally with our board of directors, our shareholders, and our lenders.

All of our budgets and actual results were focused on this number. The financial picture needed to clearly show how this number affected the cash flow of the company because everyone was so familiar with it.

- The financial picture needed to show how the timing of recording our revenues (when we billed our customers) differed from the timing of when we collected those revenues (when we received the cash). The business was highly seasonal. Because our financial statements recorded revenues on the accrual basis of accounting, certain seasonally strong months showed much higher revenues than other months. However, the cash was collected 30 to 90 days after the revenue was "earned" and recorded as revenue in our income statement.

  Our lender was always trying to get us to make a larger payment in the seasonally higher sales months. What they didn't understand was that the cash from those months did not flow into the company immediately. We could make higher payments in certain months, but not in the months they thought we should make them.

- I needed to present the other non-income statement components of the cash flow in a way that clearly showed what had happened to our cash balance and what we projected was going to happen to our cash balance. It was important to establish that we were in control of our cash flow, even though we did not have as much cash as we would have liked (or the lender would have liked us to have).

It was important that when we went to the lender and renegotiated the debt that we did not create a new payment schedule that we couldn't honor. Our credibility would be destroyed if we did that again.

What I ended up with I now call the "Peace of Mind Schedule." Looking back on it now, I ask myself, "How come I didn't come up with this schedule sooner?" I could have saved myself, and many other people associated with the company, a great deal of time and worry.

## IT MAKES PERFECT SENSE TO ME!

I knew the schedule was a winner when the vice president of the lender said to me, "This schedule is perfect. I can tell exactly what's going on with the cash. It makes perfect sense to me." He said this at the end of the meeting in our offices when we presented our proposed debt restructuring. He could see clearly where the cash had gone and where we expected it to go over the next 12 months.

The schedule was what the lender needed in order to make his decision about our proposal. He was now confident that he understood the cash flows and that the company's management was in control of the cash flow.

They gave us the new payment terms we needed.

From then on, I provided our lender with the Peace of Mind Schedule quarterly. They loved it and said they planned to have all their other companies start using it to manage and present their cash flows.

So how did we end up creating a $3.5 million profit from this lender, you ask?

Two years later, the lender's parent company wanted to get out of the business of lending money. Consequently, the subsidiary, our lender, was put up for sale.

Because they wanted to get out of the business of making loans, the lender was interested in finding creative ways to get their existing loans paid off early. Because they understood the cash flow of our company, they offered us a significant discount to pay them off. It was a deal we couldn't refuse. We were able to take advantage of their generous offer and when the deal was completed, we created a profit of $3.5 million.

This incredible deal would never have been possible if our lender hadn't felt comfortable that they understood the cash flow of our business.

The Peace of Mind Schedule presented the cash flow of the company in a way that made it clear to them where the money was going and how long it would take us to pay the loan off.

It really is the perfect tool for showing what's going on with a company's cash balance. Chapter 10 will present the schedule in a way that is simple to create and easy to understand.

# Your Action Plan

- ✔ Use the Peace of Mind Schedule to present a clear and easy-to-understand picture of your cash flow.

- ✔ Present your banker, shareholders, investors, and other key financial partners with a solid understanding of the cash flow of your business. This knowledge will do wonders to create an environment of trust and confidence with this important group of people.

- ✔ Commit to taking control of your cash flow so you can always answer the two critical cash flow questions.

# Send Me Your Questions

If you have any questions, concerns, or comments, please feel free to send them to me at pcampbell@growandsucceed.com. I respond to all my e-mail personally and promptly.

# Chapter 10

## The Peace of Mind Schedule Will Free You!

> *The whole aim of starting a business is to develop*
> *a consistent, predictable source of cash flow in excess of*
> *costs and expenses and then to hold on to the money.*
> —BRIAN TRACY, AUTHOR, MANAGEMENT EXPERT

The Peace of Mind Schedule will do for you what it has been doing for me and other business owners I have taught it to for the last 12 years—give you the peace of mind knowing you are managing the financial aspects of your business in a thoughtful and intelligent way.

The schedule is simple yet powerful. It is a complete projection of your monthly cash flow and a tool that is easy to prepare, easy to understand, and easy to maintain. It's the key to taking control of your cash flow.

In this chapter, we will take a look at the schedule and go over the components that make it unique and valuable. In Chapters 11 and 12, we will go through the step-by-step process for creating and maintaining the schedule.

These three chapters will provide you with what you need to create the Peace of Mind Schedule for your business. If someone else will be preparing and maintaining the schedule for you, share this book with them so they can prepare the schedule based on the instructions provided here.

# Seven Key Characteristics of the Peace of Mind Schedule

The Peace of Mind Schedule is set up in four sections. Exhibit 1 (at the end of Chapter 11) shows what the schedule looks like. The first page shows section 1 and the second page shows sections 2, 3, and 4 of the schedule. The schedule is designed so it can be printed using just two pieces of paper.

You can have a complete view of your cash flow over a 12-month period that fits on two pieces of paper. The schedule is designed with the K.I.S.S. (keep it simple, stupid) formula, my favorite approach to creating solutions that work.

Let's look now at the seven key characteristics that make this schedule so powerful.

## 1. Twelve Months Listed Consecutively

The schedule shows twelve months of cash flows next to each other. The first six months are actual results. The next six months are projections. There are a number of benefits to having the schedule set up this way.

First, the process of putting the last six months of actual cash flow results in the schedule helps you to see where the various components of your cash flow come from in your standard financial statements. You will learn the different places to look within your financial statements to find what you need for the schedule.

Second, creating your projections is easier when you have the last six months of activity in front of you. You have a perfect view of what the cash flow is likely to be because you have the actual cash flow results there to look at.

There is a principle you can use that will help you create consistently accurate projections. The principle simply says **the near future almost always looks a lot like the recent past.** Keep this in mind as you work with the Peace of Mind Schedule. I think you will be surprised how true this statement is in your business.

Third, you can see the ending cash balances each month on a single schedule. You can tell whether they are going up or going down each month. Are the cash balances for the coming months consistent with your goals? Are you satisfied with the cash balances you are projecting?

The schedule makes it so easy to answer these important questions about your business. It's all right there in front of you. It gives you a clear picture of what is likely to happen with your cash balance.

## 2. Your Cash Flow Is Presented Logically

The Peace of Mind Schedule presents your cash flow for the month in a logical way. Each month starts with the beginning balance, shows the different components of the cash flow for the month, and concludes with the ending cash balance. That seems like common sense, right?

One thing I learned early in my business career is this: Common sense is not so common. We all tend to be creatures of habit rather than creatures of logic. We oftentimes keep doing what we have been doing even when a better way exists.

This is especially evident with the Peace of Mind Schedule. The schedule is logical and it's easy to prepare and maintain. So why is it that only 23 percent of the businesspeople in my cash flow survey have cash flow projections?

In their book, *The CashFlow Quadrant: Rich Dad's Guide to Financial Freedom,* Robert T. Kiyosaki and Sharon L. Lechter said:

"The primary reason most people have money problems is they were never schooled in the science of cash flow management.

They were taught to read, write, drive cars, swim, but they were not taught how to manage their cash flow.

> Without this training they wind up having money problems, then work harder believing that more money will solve the problem."
>
> —*Robert T. Kiyosaki and Sharon L. Lechter, The CashFlow Quadrant: Rich Dad's Guide to Financial Freedom*

Kiyosaki and Lechter hit a big part of the problem right on the head. Most business owners have never been taught the proper way to manage the cash flow of their business.

Another reason so few business owners have cash flow projections is that many people believe the only financial schedules they need are the standard financial statements. The basic financial statements that every business must prepare *are* useful; in fact, they are a must.

The income statement, the balance sheet, and the cash flow statement are the traditional financial statements used to show the financial results of any business. Banks as well as investors require you to provide them. They are the common language of business.

The problem is that the financial statements are always historical, meaning they are focused on presenting what happened in the past. This is critical financial information. However, you must also have a tool for projecting your cash flow into the future.

You need to know what your financial results were in prior months, what your balances are right now, and what you expect your cash balance to be over at least the next six months.

The basic financial statements take care of the first two requirements. The Peace of Mind Schedule will take care of the third.

## Choose the Right Tool for the Job

Another trait of the basic financial statements that causes confusion is the statement called the "Cash Flow Statement." Its name suggests that it would be the perfect tool to use to manage your cash flow.

**It's not!**

The basic problem with the Cash Flow Statement is the format and approach used to create it. It basically "backs into" the change in the cash balance during the period being presented.

It takes net income as reported on the income statement and then computes changes in a number of balance sheet accounts, together with other investing and financing activities, to arrive at the change in the cash balance for the period.

I heard it described recently by an MBA student. I was standing in line with a young woman at a seminar. She told me she had just completed her last accounting course as part of her MBA program.

I began talking about how **Cash Is King** and how it's so important in business to make sure you have your cash flow under control. (I couldn't pass up the opportunity to help her get off to a good start!)

She said, "Yeah, in the last part of the course we learned about the cash flow statement. That was hard. It's like working backward."

What a perfect description. That's why it is not the right tool for cash flow projections. The Cash Flow Statement is formatted to work backward from net income to the change in the cash balance.

Abraham Maslow, a well-known writer, had a great saying that fits this subject.

"When all you have is a hammer, everything starts to look like a nail."

—*Abraham Maslow*

A hammer is a useful tool when you need to drive nails. When you need to cut a board, though, the hammer is not the proper tool.

If you work long enough and hard enough, you might be able to break the board with the hammer. The problem is you will have a splintered board. You will have done something worse than if you had never used the hammer on it at all.

It's the same way with the cash flow statement that is a part of the basic financial statements. Don't try to use it as a tool for managing your cash flow. That's not what it was designed to do.

So the rule here is to continue to provide the cash flow statement as a part of the basic financial statements to your bankers, investors, partners, and so on. Anyone who wants a full set of your basic financial statements should get them. However, to manage your cash flow each month, use the Peace of Mind Schedule. It's the right tool for answering the question, "What do I expect my cash balance to be six months from now?"

## 3. Revenues and Expenses Agree with Your Income Statement

Section 1 of the schedule comes right off your income statement. You simply enter the revenues and expenses just as they are shown on your income statement.

It's important to note here that most financial statements are prepared on the accrual basis of accounting. Although it's not important for you to have an in-depth knowledge of accrual basis accounting, it is important to walk through the basics. This will help you see why having section 1 of the schedule come directly from your income statement makes the schedule easy to use and maintain.

The two primary methods of accounting are cash basis accounting and accrual basis accounting.

Cash basis accounting is basically what its name implies. It says you record revenues when you receive money and you record expenses when you pay money (with a number of exceptions—inventory being one of them). Many small businesses use this method of accounting.

Accrual basis accounting says you record revenues in your income statement when the revenues are earned, not when you receive the money. It also says you record expenses when the expenses are incurred, not when they are paid. All medium to large businesses (and many small businesses) use this method of accounting.

Here is an example of the difference in the two methods. Suppose you provide a service to a customer for $500. You provide the service on May 25th and send them an invoice on May 26th for the $500. You actually receive the $500 from your customer on June 30th.

If your books were maintained on the accrual basis of accounting, your income statement would show the $500 as revenue in the month of May. Even though you did not receive the money until June, the revenue was earned in May. Therefore, it is recorded as revenue in your income statement in May.

If your books were maintained on the cash basis, your income statement would show the $500 as revenue in the month of June. It would not show any revenue related to this customer invoice until you actually received the cash.

Regardless of the method of accounting you use, section 1 of the Peace of Mind Schedule comes right off your income statement. Section 4 of the schedule includes several lines that take into account the primary differences between the revenue and expenses in an income statement prepared on the accrual basis of accounting and the timing of the actual cash receipts and disbursements.

### 4. Your EBITDA as the Primary Measure of Operating Cash Flow

Section 1 of the schedule comes down to EBITDA. This is your *E*arnings *B*efore *I*nterest, *T*axes, *D*epreciation, and *A*mortization. It is basically a measure of your operating cash flow.

The income statement that is part of the basic financial statements shows revenues and expenses and calculates the difference as operating income. It also deducts interest expense and taxes in order to arrive at net income.

All you do when you are entering the numbers from your income statement into the Peace of Mind Schedule is to enter all the revenues and expenses *except* interest, taxes, depreciation, and amortization.

The schedule then computes EBITDA, which is a good measure of your operating cash flow for the month. It is basically the cash your business generated (or used) for normal operations.

## 5. Cash You Use for Debt Service

This section is where you put your debt service payments. These are the payments you make on loans with the bank or other financial institution or person who has loaned you money.

The amount here is the total payment. Both principal and interest are included so it is clear how much of your cash is leaving your business for the purpose of servicing loans.

Any borrowings you receive in a particular month would also be included in this section.

## 6. Cash You Invest in the Business

This section of the schedule is quite simple. This is where you enter the cash you invested in your business during the month you are working on.

The most common item in this section would be capital expenditures. For example, suppose you just wrote a check for $10,000 for a new vehicle for your delivery business. The cost of the vehicle will have been recorded on your balance sheet rather than as an expense in your income statement. Therefore, it will not have been shown in section 1 of the schedule because it is not considered an expense when you bought it. It is an investment in your business. We will talk more in the next chapter about where to get the numbers that you will enter in this section of the Peace of Mind Schedule.

## 7. Other Cash Flow Items and Timing Differences

This section is what makes the schedule so unique and powerful. This part of the schedule is primarily focused on capturing the various "timing differences" created in your income statement by the accrual basis of accounting.

We discussed earlier in the chapter how the accrual basis of accounting requires certain revenues and expenses to be recognized in a month different from when the actual money is received or paid out. Those "timing differences" are taken into account here to show the actual impact on your cash balance.

One of the benefits you will notice from this section of the schedule is how it helps you see the effect those differences have on the timing of your actual cash receipts and disbursements. You will find that you begin to better understand what's really going on with your cash balance when you can see in one place exactly how those "timing differences" impact your cash flow and your ending cash balance each month.

Now that we have covered the key characteristics that make the Peace of Mind Schedule so unique and powerful, let's take the next step. We will go through the step-by-step process for creating the schedule.

Repeat after me: "There is no better time than now to take control of my cash flow! There is no better time than now to take control of my cash flow! There is no better time than now to take control of my cash flow!"

---

## The 10 Cash Flow Rules

### *Rule #10*
## Eliminate Your Cash Flow Worries So You Are Free to Do What You Do Best—Grow Your Business and Make More Money

---

# Your Action Plan

✔ The near future almost always looks a lot like the recent past. Use this principle to help you create cash flow projections you can trust.

✔ Six months of actual cash flows next to six months of projected cash flows is a wonderful way to see clearly where the cash has been and where it's going. Commit now to take control of your cash flow by creating the Peace of Mind Schedule—**now.**

✔ Take the time to fully understand the key cash flow "timing differences" in your business. It will help you understand and successfully manage your cash flow.

# Send Me Your Questions

If you have any questions, concerns, or comments, please feel free to send them to me at pcampbell@growandsucceed.com. I respond to all my e-mail personally and promptly.

# Chapter 11

## Putting the Peace of Mind Schedule to Work

*Spectacular achievements are always*
*preceded by painstaking preparation.*
—ROGER STAUBACH, BUSINESSMAN, FORMER
DALLAS COWBOY QUARTERBACK

In this chapter I will show you the step-by-step process for creating and maintaining the Peace of Mind Schedule.

Just a reminder that if you will have someone else prepare and maintain the schedule for you, share this book with that person so he or she can prepare the schedule based on the instructions provided.

Like anything else of value in life or business, there is some work involved. The schedule requires a little effort to make it effective.

I think you will find, though, that what you learn in the process of creating the schedule (especially seeing 12 months of cash flows together for the first time) will make it more than worthwhile. You will have insight into your cash flow that you have never had before.

Maintaining the schedule after it is created is quite easy.

First, let's go through the steps to create the schedule, and then go through the steps for maintaining it each month.

# Creating the Peace of Mind Schedule

### 1. Set Up the Spreadsheet

The Peace of Mind Schedule is designed to be created and maintained as an electronic spreadsheet. You can create a spreadsheet by using the Exhibit Schedule at the end of this chapter as a guide. Then, simply set the schedule up in your favorite spreadsheet software.

If you would like to avoid setting the schedule up from scratch, you're in luck. You can get a preformatted Excel file for **FREE.** Here is how to get it:

- Go to www.neverrunoutofcash.com/freetools.htm and click on the link to provide me with your feedback and comments about the book.

- After providing me with your valuable comments and feedback, you will be able to download the Peace of Mind Schedule— **FREE!** (It is an Excel spreadsheet file—you need to have Excel or compatible software to open the file.)

- The schedule will be set up and ready for you to use. *Take just a minute* to complete the short feedback form and get the Peace of Mind Schedule.

### 2. Make Changes to Track Your Income Statement

The Peace of Mind Schedule shown in Exhibit 1 has some generic revenue and expense categories. You will need to change these to be the same as the revenue and expense categories in your income statement.

You want the schedule to track your income statement format as closely as possible, so enter your revenues and expenses in the schedule exactly as they appear in your existing income statement. This helps make sure your cash flow projections are easy to create, easy to maintain, and easy to understand.

## 3. Enter the Previous Six Months' Cash Flow Data

Now it's time to bring the schedule to life. Entering the last six months of actual results is a great way to begin the process. It's amazing how seeing each month's results side-by-side will help you understand your cash flow.

To get started, gather your financial statements for each of the last seven months (you will need that seventh month to get your beginning cash balance). For example, suppose it is July 25th. Your last six months of financial statements would be the months January through June. These are the months you will be entering in the schedule.

Therefore, you would gather your financial statements for December of the previous year and January through June of the current year. The reason you need December is that the ending cash balance for December will be entered in the schedule as the beginning balance for January.

### Section 1—Your Income Statement

Enter the December ending cash balance from your balance sheet as the beginning cash balance for January.

Now enter the revenue and expenses for January from your income statement. Enter revenues and expenses both as positive numbers.

The schedule will automatically treat expense amounts as deductions from EBITDA and the cash balance.

If you are creating the schedule yourself, set the formulas up so the expense items in this section are treated as deductions from cash flow.

After entering your income statement information, go back and make sure the EBITDA amount that the schedule calculates is accurate. Check each of the revenue and expense categories back to your income statement to make sure it was all entered correctly.

## Section 2—Cash You Use for Debt Service

Enter your debt service payments for the month in this section. These are the payments you make on loans with your bank or other financial institution or person who has loaned you money. The amount you enter here should be the total payments. This includes both principal and interest—the total of all payments made on loans or other debt.

Enter payments in this section as a negative number. If you borrowed any money during the period, you would enter that as a positive number. The best place to get this information is from your payment records. No need to worry about separating the interest from the principal. Simply enter the total payments you made on loans for that month.

## Section 3—Cash You Invest in the Business

Enter the amount of actual cash outlays that represent investments in your business for the month in this section.

The most common item here is capital expenditures. Your general ledger is the best place to find the amount of cash you actually spent for assets that must be capitalized (recorded on the balance sheet rather than expensed when purchased).

Enter amounts you invested in the business as a negative number. If you sold an asset during the period, you would enter the proceeds as a positive number.

If you are unsure how to get this number, ask your accountant or CPA to provide the number for you each month. It will save you the time of looking through the detailed general ledger to find the amount for the month.

## Section 4—Other Cash Flow Items

This section of the schedule is primarily focused on capturing the various "timing differences" created in your income statement by the accrual basis of accounting.

We discussed in Chapter 10 how the accrual basis of accounting requires certain revenues and expenses to be recognized in a month different from when the money is actually received or paid out. Those "timing differences" are taken into account here in order to show the actual impact your results had on your cash balance.

This section of the schedule is extremely important. It's the key to really understanding the difference between financial results as presented in your financial statements (especially the income statement) and the actual impact your business decisions had, and will have, on your cash balance.

Let's discuss each line in section 4 of the schedule.

*Deduct: sales*—This line takes the sales amount in section 1 of the schedule and deducts it here. The purpose of deducting those sales now is to account for the fact that some sales are recorded as revenue in the income statement prior to being collected as cash.

The schedule deducts sales as recorded in section 1, then uses the next line in the schedule to add back all cash receipts related to sales or the collection of accounts receivable. This approach works whether you use the cash basis of accounting or the accrual basis of accounting.

If you use the cash basis of accounting, then the next line in the schedule will just add your sales back in because your sales would be the same as the cash you collected.

If you use the accrual basis of accounting, this line is crucial because the sales as recorded in your income statement will not be the same as the cash you collect related to sales for the month or amounts you collect on your existing accounts receivable.

Let's look back briefly at the example from Chapter 10. In that example, you provided a service to a customer for $500 on May 25th and sent them an invoice on May 26th for that amount. You didn't actually receive the $500 from your customer until the end of June.

Under the accrual basis of accounting, your income statement would show the $500 as revenue in the month of May. At that time the impact on your cash balance would be zero.

Even though you did not receive the money until June, the revenue was earned in May. Therefore, it is recorded as revenue in your income statement in May.

*Add: cash collected from sales and accounts receivable*—This is the line where you enter the total cash collected for sales during the month and for collections on your accounts receivable.

The previous line deducted sales as recorded in the income statement. This line adds back all the cash collected in the month regardless of the period in which those sales appeared in the income statement.

*Add: cost of goods sold*—This line takes the cost of goods sold from section 1 and adds it back into your cash flow. The assumption here is that cost of goods sold in your income statement may or may not be the same as the cash you actually spent to buy the products you sell.

For example, suppose you have a retail business selling home furnishings. In July, you buy a framed picture for $100 to sell in your business. You pay for the picture in July and hang it on the wall to sell. In September, you sell the picture for $600. (If you are going to run a business, you might as well make good money, right?)

In your July financial statements you cannot deduct the $100 as a cost of goods sold because it was not sold in July. When you bought the picture, you increased your inventory by $100. On the books, the $100 was recorded in the inventory account on your balance sheet.

In September, your sales line would include the $600 selling price of the picture. The cost of goods sold line in your income statement for September would include the $100 cost of the picture you sold. The revenue from selling the picture and the related cost of the picture appear in the income statement in the same month the inventory was sold.

The $100 purchase in July would show up in the Peace of Mind Schedule in July on the inventory purchases line (we will talk about that line next). In September, it would appear in your cost of goods sold as an expense and would be added back on the line called "Add: cost of goods sold."

This way the schedule has made the adjustments necessary to take into account the impact this inventory purchase has on your cash balance. The impact it has on your cash balance and the impact it has on your income statement happen in different months.

*Deduct: inventory purchases*—This line is where you record your inventory purchases for the month. Enter the amount on this line as a negative number.

The previous line added back the cost of goods sold regardless of when the inventory that was sold was purchased.

This line deducts all your inventory purchases for the month regardless of whether any of it was sold in that month or not. Therefore, you are reflecting the actual impact on your cash balance. This approach greatly simplifies the process of creating and maintaining the schedule.

You can find the dollar amount of your inventory purchases in your general ledger. How you, or your accountant or CPA, record inventory purchases in the general ledger determines whether you can find it in one account or in multiple accounts. Either way, your inventory purchases for the month should be easy to get from your financials or your general ledger.

*Estimated tax payments*—Here is where you include any estimated tax payments you make during the month. Enter the amounts here as a negative number.

*Change in accounts payable*—The amount you enter on this line is the difference between your accounts payable balance at the end of this month minus the accounts payable balance at the end of the previous month. It is simply a calculation right off your financial statements (from the balance sheet).

The purpose of this line is to adjust for the effect the accrual basis of accounting has on the recording of expenses. This accounting method requires that expenses be recorded in the income statement when they are incurred, not when they are paid.

When an expense is recorded prior to being paid, the accounts payable balance on your balance sheet is increased by the amount of the expense. When it is paid, the accounts payable balance is reduced (as well as the cash balance being reduced) by the amount of the payment.

If the accounts payable balance has increased from the prior month, that means more expenses have been recorded (accrued) than have actually been paid.

On the other hand, if the accounts payable balance has declined from the prior month, that means more of your bills have been paid than have been recorded as an expense in your income statement.

Let's look at an example to help illustrate how this works.

Suppose you had a graphics designer create a newsletter for your business. The total cost for the service was $150.

The work was completed and you received the newsletter on May 10th and you received the invoice for $150 from the designer on May 20th. You actually pay the invoice on June 10th.

Under the accrual basis of accounting, your income statement would show the $150 as an expense in the month of May. But the impact on your cash balance in May would be zero because you didn't pay the invoice until June.

Even though you did not pay the money until June, the expense was incurred in May. Therefore, it is recorded as an expense in your income statement in May.

This line of the Peace of Mind Schedule makes sure that these "timing differences" in your income statement are adjusted to show the impact they have on your actual cash flow and your cash balance.

*Other*—Two lines are labeled "other." They provide you the flexibility to relabel them if you have a specific item you would like to capture here. If you have prepaid rent, deposits, or other prepaid expenses you can show those here.

It can also be used as a "miscellaneous" line. This is the net activity of any cash flow timing difference not specifically designated in a separate line on the schedule.

*Net cash flow*—This line is a formula that computes your net cash flow for the month. This shows you whether you brought in more cash than you sent out (that's good) or whether it turned out the other way around (that's bad).

Focus in on this line as you review the actual cash flow results and as you prepare your projections. This is an important number to know. It shows you whether you are moving in the right direction or not.

*Ending cash balance*—This line is a formula that takes the beginning balance for the month and either adds or subtracts your net cash flow for the month. The result is your cash balance at the end of that month.

At this point, you have entered one month of your actual cash flows in the Peace of Mind Schedule. The quickest way to make sure the numbers are accurate is to make sure the ending cash balance for the month in the schedule agrees with the ending cash balance on your balance sheet for that month. Your balance sheet provides your asset, liability, and equity account balances at the end of any given month.

When you enter your results in the Peace of Mind schedule, you are not finished with the month you are entering until you have made sure the ending cash balance on the schedule agrees to the same cash balance on your balance sheet.

*Minimum cash balance target*—This line serves as a reminder that you need to have a certain minimum cash balance at the end of each month. You need to have enough cash on hand at the end of the month to get the bills paid that are due very early in the next month. This is especially important if your cash receipts tend to come in toward the middle or end of each month.

The number you use here is really a matter of deciding what minimum level of cash balance you are comfortable with. If you are not sure what the minimum amount should be, a rule of thumb you can use is to have at least two weeks' worth of operating expenses available. You could take your total operating expenses from section 2 of the schedule and multiply that number times .5.

In the example schedule, you will notice that the $8,000 minimum cash balance target is almost 2 months' worth of total operating expenses. Remember, this line is just meant to help you think through the minimum end of month cash balance you are comfortable with. You can set it at whatever amount you feel is appropriate.

You can also use this line to set a target for where you want to see your cash balance. You can set it much higher than the minimum cash you need and use it as a reminder of what your goals are for growing your cash balance over time.

*Cash excess (shortfall)*—This line takes the ending cash balance and subtracts the minimum cash balance target. A positive number means your ending cash balance for that month is above the minimum level you set for the business. That's good.

If this line shows a negative number, then your ending cash balance is below the minimum cash level you set. That's bad. This will require you to think through all the implications of being short of cash and create a very specific list of action steps you can take to fix, or at least mitigate, the problem.

# Exhibit 1
## Cash Is King, Inc.
## The Peace of Mind Schedule
Year: _____

| | | | | | | Example Schedule | | | | | | | |
|---|---|---|---|---|---|---|---|---|---|---|---|---|---|
| | Jan | Feb | Mar | Apr | May | Jun | Jul | Aug | Sep | Oct | Nov | Dec | Year |
| Beginning cash balance | $10,000 | $10,905 | $15,605 | $21,230 | $23,235 | $27,340 | $30,845 | $32,100 | $36,105 | $40,110 | $41,115 | $44,870 | $10,000 |
| **Section 1** | | | | | | | | | | | | | |
| **Revenues** | | | | | | | | | | | | | |
| Sales | 15,000 | 13,000 | 14,500 | 15,000 | 15,000 | 15,000 | 15,000 | 15,000 | 15,000 | 15,000 | 15,000 | 15,000 | 177,500 |
| Other | 0 | 0 | 0 | 0 | 0 | 0 | 0 | 0 | 0 | 0 | 0 | 0 | 0 |
| Total | 15,000 | 13,000 | 14,500 | 15,000 | 15,000 | 15,000 | 15,000 | 15,000 | 15,000 | 15,000 | 15,000 | 15,000 | 177,500 |
| Cost of goods sold | 3,750 | 3,250 | 3,625 | 3,750 | 3,750 | 3,750 | 3,750 | 3,750 | 3,750 | 3,750 | 3,750 | 3,750 | 44,375 |
| Gross profit | 11,250 | 9,750 | 10,875 | 11,250 | 11,250 | 11,250 | 11,250 | 11,250 | 11,250 | 11,250 | 11,250 | 11,250 | 133,125 |
| **Operating expenses** | | | | | | | | | | | | | |
| Compensation, benefits, and taxes | 2,000 | 2,100 | 2,050 | 2,200 | 1,900 | 2,000 | 2,000 | 2,000 | 2,000 | 2,000 | 2,000 | 2,000 | 24,250 |
| Rent | 1,000 | 1,000 | 1,000 | 1,000 | 1,000 | 1,000 | 1,000 | 1,000 | 1,000 | 1,000 | 1,000 | 1,000 | 12,000 |
| Advertising and marketing | 600 | 1,000 | 400 | 400 | 600 | 600 | 600 | 600 | 600 | 600 | 600 | 600 | 7,200 |
| Insurance | 200 | 200 | 200 | 200 | 200 | 200 | 200 | 200 | 200 | 200 | 200 | 200 | 2,400 |
| Repairs and maintenance | 50 | 50 | 50 | 50 | 50 | 50 | 50 | 50 | 50 | 50 | 50 | 50 | 600 |
| Legal and accounting | 300 | 300 | 300 | 300 | 300 | 300 | 300 | 300 | 300 | 300 | 300 | 300 | 3,600 |
| Telephone and utilities | 150 | 150 | 150 | 150 | 150 | 150 | 150 | 150 | 150 | 150 | 150 | 150 | 1,800 |
| Travel, meals, and entertainment | 120 | 50 | 150 | 120 | 120 | 120 | 120 | 120 | 120 | 120 | 120 | 120 | 1,400 |
| Office supplies and expenses | 75 | 75 | 150 | 75 | 75 | 75 | 75 | 75 | 75 | 75 | 75 | 75 | 900 |
| Dues and subscriptions | 75 | 150 | 100 | 75 | 75 | 75 | 75 | 75 | 75 | 75 | 75 | 75 | 1,000 |
| Miscellaneous | 200 | 200 | 200 | 200 | 200 | 200 | 200 | 200 | 200 | 200 | 200 | 200 | 2,400 |
| Total | 4,770 | 5,275 | 4,675 | 4,770 | 4,670 | 4,770 | 4,770 | 4,770 | 4,770 | 4,770 | 4,770 | 4,770 | 57,550 |
| EBITDA | $ 6,480 | $ 4,475 | $ 6,200 | $ 6,480 | $ 6,580 | $ 6,480 | $ 6,480 | $ 6,480 | $ 6,480 | $ 6,480 | $ 6,480 | $ 6,480 | $75,575 |

# Exhibit 1 (continued)

## Section 2
### Debt service (principal and interest)

| | Jan | Feb | Mar | Apr | May | Jun | Jul | Aug | Sep | Oct | Nov | Dec | Year |
|---|---|---|---|---|---|---|---|---|---|---|---|---|---|
| Note 1 | (1,100) | (1,100) | (1,100) | (1,100) | (1,100) | (1,100) | (1,100) | (1,100) | (1,100) | (1,100) | (1,100) | (1,100) | (13,200) |
| Note 2 | 0 | 0 | 0 | 0 | 0 | 0 | 0 | 0 | 0 | 0 | 0 | 0 | 0 |
| Other | 0 | 0 | 0 | 0 | 0 | 0 | 0 | 0 | 0 | 0 | 0 | 0 | 0 |
| Totals | (1,100) | (1,100) | (1,100) | (1,100) | (1,100) | (1,100) | (1,100) | (1,100) | (1,100) | (1,100) | (1,100) | (1,100) | (13,200) |

## Section 3
### Investments

| | Jan | Feb | Mar | Apr | May | Jun | Jul | Aug | Sep | Oct | Nov | Dec | Year |
|---|---|---|---|---|---|---|---|---|---|---|---|---|---|
| Capital expenditures | (100) | (1,500) | 0 | 0 | 0 | (500) | 0 | 0 | 0 | 0 | (250) | 0 | (2,350) |
| Other | 0 | 0 | 0 | 0 | 0 | 0 | 0 | 0 | 0 | 0 | 0 | 0 | 0 |
| Totals | (100) | (1,500) | 0 | 0 | 0 | (500) | 0 | 0 | 0 | 0 | (250) | 0 | (2,350) |

## Section 4
### Other cash flow items and timing differences

| | Jan | Feb | Mar | Apr | May | Jun | Jul | Aug | Sep | Oct | Nov | Dec | Year |
|---|---|---|---|---|---|---|---|---|---|---|---|---|---|
| Deduct: sales | (15,000) | (13,000) | (14,500) | (15,000) | (15,000) | (15,000) | (15,000) | (15,000) | (15,000) | (15,000) | (15,000) | (15,000) | (177,500) |
| Add: cash collected from sales and A/R | 14,500 | 15,500 | 15,000 | 14,500 | 14,500 | 14,500 | 14,500 | 14,500 | 14,500 | 14,500 | 14,500 | 14,500 | 175,500 |
| Add: cost of goods sold | 3,750 | 3,250 | 3,625 | 3,750 | 3,750 | 3,750 | 3,750 | 3,750 | 3,750 | 3,750 | 3,750 | 3,750 | 44,375 |
| Deduct: inventory purchases | (4,125) | (2,925) | (4,350) | (4,125) | (4,125) | (4,125) | (4,125) | (4,125) | (4,125) | (4,125) | (4,125) | (4,125) | (48,525) |
| Estimated tax payments | (3,000) | 0 | 0 | (2,500) | 0 | (2,750) | 0 | 0 | 0 | (3,000) | 0 | 0 | (11,250) |
| Change in accounts payable | (500) | 0 | 750 | 0 | (500) | (500) | (500) | (500) | (500) | (500) | (500) | (500) | (3,750) |
| Other | 0 | 0 | 0 | 0 | 0 | 0 | 0 | 0 | 0 | 0 | 0 | 0 | 0 |
| Totals | (4,375) | 2,825 | 525 | (3,375) | (1,375) | (1,375) | (4,125) | (1,375) | (1,375) | (4,375) | (1,375) | (1,375) | (21,150) |
| Net cash flow | 905 | 4,700 | 5,625 | 2,005 | 4,105 | 3,505 | 1,255 | 4,005 | 4,005 | 1,005 | 3,755 | 4,005 | 38,875 |
| Ending cash balance | $10,905 | $15,605 | $21,230 | $23,235 | $27,340 | $30,845 | $32,100 | $36,105 | $40,110 | $41,115 | $44,870 | $48,875 | $48,875 |
| Minimum cash balance target | $8,000 | $8,000 | $8,000 | $8,000 | $8,000 | $8,000 | $8,000 | $8,000 | $8,000 | $8,000 | $8,000 | $8,000 | $8,000 |
| Cash excess (shortfall) | $2,905 | $7,605 | $13,230 | $15,235 | $19,340 | $22,845 | $24,100 | $28,105 | $32,110 | $33,115 | $36,870 | $40,875 | $40,875 |

# ENTERING THE MOST RECENT SIX MONTHS OF ACTUAL CASH FLOWS

Now that you have the first month entered in the schedule, it's time to enter the next five months. This way the schedule will have your most recent six months of actual cash flows.

Having six months of actual cash flows side-by-side will be both revealing and insightful. It also makes the process of creating your projections easier. We will go over the process of creating the projections in Chapter 12.

Take the time now to enter the next five months of actual results.

As you enter each month, you will notice that the ending cash balance for the month you just entered is automatically entered as the beginning balance for the next month.

Other than the beginning balance, the process is exactly the same as you used to enter the first month of cash flow results. Follow that same process to enter the remaining five months of actual results into the Peace of Mind Schedule.

# EITHER YOU DO THE WORK OR HAVE SOMEONE ELSE DO IT

This is a good time to look back on Cash Flow Rule #5.

You should be able to find the complete list of The 10 Cash Flow Rules on your bathroom mirror. (If you're not sure why they would be on your bathroom mirror, then it's time reread Chapter 3.)

Cash Flow Rule #5 will help you make sure the work that needs to get done actually gets done. It's not enough to know what to do. What counts is what actually gets done.

In this case, you need to set up the Peace of Mind Schedule and enter the most recent six months of actual cash flows. There is no question that it requires a little work and effort to get started.

There is definitely work that needs to be done. That is where Cash Flow Rule #5 will help you. This cash flow rule will help you make sure today's work gets done today.

The rule says:

1. You do the work

   or

2. You have someone else do the work.

You have only two choices. The work must be done. The schedule must be set up so you can take control of your cash flow. Someone has to do it, which means either you do it or you have someone else do it.

If you are creating the schedule yourself, take the time to set it up, enter the last six months of actual cash flows, and project the next six months. If you will have your accountant, CPA, or someone else in your company set the schedule up for you, great. Share this book with them, communicate your performance standards, then make sure it gets done.

I guarantee you the Peace of Mind Schedule will become a tool you will never want to be without. It will transform the way you manage your business.

---

### The 10 Cash Flow Rules

*Rule #5*
### Either You Do the Work or Have Someone Else Do It

# Your Action Plan

✔ Commit to take control of your cash flow by creating the Peace of Mind Schedule—**NOW.**

✔ You can get a preformatted Peace of Mind Schedule (an Excel spreadsheet file) FREE. Go to www.neverrunoutofcash.com/freetools.htm, provide me with your valuable comments and feedback on the book, and you will be able to download the schedule. This will save you the time of creating the schedule from scratch. Take a minute now to provide your feedback and download the schedule.

✔ If you will not be creating the schedule yourself, decide **now** who you will have complete the schedule for you. Then make sure the work gets done.

# Send Me Your Questions

If you have any questions, concerns, or comments, please feel free to send them to me at pcampbell@growandsucceed.com. I respond to all my e-mail personally and promptly.

# Chapter 12

## Cash Flow Projections the Right Way

*It's better to be approximately right than precisely wrong.*
—Boyd Plowman, Chief Financial Officer,
Fleetwood Enterprises, Inc.

By the end of this chapter, you will have the information you need to answer the critical cash flow question—What do I expect my cash balance to be six months from now?

You will have taken a huge step toward taking control of your cash flow. You will be managing your business rather than letting it manage you.

It's so much easier to analyze alternative strategies and make better business decisions when you have the facts. You won't wonder whether you can actually honor the financial commitments you want to make (or have already made). Having the answers to this critical cash flow question will help you "focus forward." It will help you make wise and profitable decisions about your business.

I once had someone say to me: "There is no guarantee that any business decision I make will be profitable. Even if I have good information and I have my cash flow under control, there is still no guarantee I will be successful."

My response to that statement was, "That's true. There is some risk inherent in every business decision. That's a part of the reality of business."

The key, though, is to always focus on ways to increase the likelihood that your business decisions are profitable. Successful people work on ways to put the odds of success in their favor. They are keenly focused on learning and growing so they continually get better at making money.

That's the reason it's so important to have your cash flow under control.

Successful people know where they stand and where they are headed. They recognize that cash is a precious asset. Knowing what the cash balance is right now and what it is expected to be six months from now is a critical component of their success in business.

It's a critical component of your success, too.

## Cash Flow Projections Made Easy

Creating cash flow projections does not have to be a difficult process. It is really a matter of using a few basic principles together with your intuition and knowledge about the business.

Here is the four step process for creating accurate projections that will make it much easier for you to make better business decisions each day.

### 1. The Near Future Almost Always Looks a Lot Like the Recent Past

Creating your projections is much easier when you have the last six months of activity right there in front of you. You have insight into what the cash flow is likely to be because you have the last six months of actual cash flow results there to look at.

You will be amazed at how this principle will help you create accurate projections. It also makes the process easier and faster for you.

The starting point to putting this principle to work is to take time to look at the six months of actual cash flows you have entered in the schedule.

Have the revenues and expenses been coming in the way you expected them to? Can you see a trend developing? Are you surprised by any of the numbers now that you are looking at the last six months of actual results next to each other?

I analyzed a large company's cash flow where this step really helped the owner get a handle on his financial situation. At the same time he came to better understand the financial implications of the way he managed the business.

He was quite surprised (and a bit irritated) when he reviewed the Peace of Mind Schedule I prepared for him. He said: "There is no way our projected cash balance could be so low. We have been cutting costs for the last three months. In fact, we are still cutting some of those costs. The projected costs are too high."

He had issued a mandate to his vice presidents in the field about four months prior to reduce costs. He then had a conference call with them each week after that to discuss progress. During the call, the vice presidents discussed the cost reductions they had identified and were putting in place. He got plenty of positive feedback from them about the costs they were cutting. He got a lot of good news each week on the conference call.

The problem was the actual results for the company did not show that costs were coming down. They had been basically flat for the last six months. As a result, I prepared the projections for him on the assumption the near future would look a lot like the recent past.

Although the vice presidents had reduced some costs, the majority of changes they were making were shifting costs from one area of the company to another. Certain costs were actually going up at the same time, which offset the savings. The owner was hearing the good news part of the story. He was not hearing the whole story.

In that process, he learned why it is so important to look at the last six months of actual results to see if the numbers are coming in the way you think they should. He thought costs should be coming down, but a quick look at the results clearly showed they were not. As a result, the projections had to be prepared based on what was *actually* happening, not what he thought *should* be happening.

Always keep this principle in mind as you work with the Peace of Mind Schedule—the near future almost always looks a lot like the recent past.

### 2. Consider What Is Changing

Is anything in the business changing right now in a significant way?

If you just negotiated a 10 percent discount in the cost of a product you re-sell to your customers, then you should consider whether it should be reflected in the month you will experience the reduced cost. The key here is to make sure it is significant enough that you are certain of its impact. Otherwise, it would be better to see the impact in your actual results before including it in your projections.

If you just hired a person in your marketing department, then make sure this additional cost is reflected in your projections.

### 3. Be Conservative

One thing about a projection you can be certain of: it will not be perfectly accurate. You can be 100 percent certain that the actual results will vary somewhat from what you project. The trick is to get close.

It's like meeting someone for lunch. You agree to meet a good friend at a restaurant at 12:00 noon. You set 12:00 as the time to meet so you will both be there at about the same time. You set a specific time so there is no confusion.

Despite the precise time you set, you know that both of you will not show up at exactly 12:00. The only question is whether you will be there a little before 12:00 or a little after 12:00. Will you be early or will you be late?

It's the same with projections. Your estimates will not be perfectly accurate. Despite that fact, you still have to pick a number that you think will be close.

You could go so far as to say the actual cash balance will definitely not turn out to be exactly what you projected it to be; the same way you will seldom ever arrive at the restaurant to meet your friend for lunch at exactly the time you agree to.

What's important is to be close—and to err on the side of being conservative. In the lunch example, would you want to be a little early or a little late? Which is the more prudent approach?

My answer to that question is it's always better to be a little early. Being late will irritate your friend. It will hurt your relationship with the other person (especially if you make a habit of it). Erring on the side of being late is a poor decision that does nothing but create ill will.

With cash flow projections, you want to err on the side of being conservative. You want to miss the cash balance on the low side. That way the surprise is pleasant rather than unpleasant.

Think about the benefits you create for yourself by having cash flow projections. One of the primary benefits is to see cash flow problems before they happen. If you see a problem with the cash balance at the end of any month you are projecting, you have just taken the first step toward making sure the problem does not actually happen.

You have made it clear a problem is looming and you have identified exactly how much of a problem it may be. You have put a dollar value on the problem. This is step 1 in the process of prevention.

The following example will help make this point clearer.

A business owner I worked with had just completed the process of creating her cash flow projections and putting them in the Peace of Mind Schedule. Her first month of projected cash flow was May.

She had already entered her actual results for the months of November through April (the last six months). And she had also entered the projected cash flows for the months of May through October.

She had a one-time payment of $10,000 due in August. It was a balloon payment on a loan she made two years ago to purchase new equipment. It was set up with a balloon payment at the end of the term in order to keep the monthly payments down.

Her projected cash balance at the end of August was $4,000. The good news was the projection showed she would be able to make the $10,000 balloon payment and still have a positive cash balance at the end of August. The bad news was the $4,000 projected ending cash balance was not a big enough balance to give her a feeling of security. It was too close to zero.

## THE 90 PERCENT TEST

This is the point in the process where she had to stop and ask herself the question, "Have I been conservative in my projections?"

Here is a simple test that will bring you amazing results. I call it the 90 Percent Test.

Are you 90 percent sure the cash balances will come in at or better than you projected? The key here is the phrase "at or better than you projected." If you can answer yes to this question with confidence, then your projections are sufficiently conservative.

The 90 Percent Test will help make sure you err on the side of being conservative with your projections.

The business owner put her projections to the 90 Percent Test. She could not answer yes with confidence because she felt uncomfortable with the revenue projections for June, July, and August. She was comfortable with the expense projections, but not quite secure with her revenues.

The common mistake business owners make when projecting revenues is they have a tendency to project them too high. Most people have

a tendency to let their optimism and confidence in their product or service run a little wild when they are projecting revenues into the future.

She projected revenues for each month that looked like this:

June        $21,000
July        $22,500
August      $23,500

Her actual average monthly sales for November through April were
$20,500. The reason she initially projected June through August with
such an increase was that she had a new marketing plan and was optimistic
it would produce higher sales. The plan was to begin the first week of June.

Is it a good idea to project that a new program will be successful
before it is even launched? Is it a good idea to take the opposite
approach and assume it will do nothing to increase sales?

The answer is no to the first question and maybe to the second
question.

The approach that works best here is to never build into your
projections a revenue increase until you see the increase in your
actual results. This way you have evidence that what you are doing
to increase revenues is working. When you see the higher revenues
in your financial results, you know it is working.

You can then more intelligently and more accurately project the
coming months based on what you are actually experiencing.

After reviewing the situation, here is what she decided to do.
She revised her revenue projections as follows:

|         | Original Projection | Conservative Projection | Difference |
|---------|--------------------|-----------------------|------------|
| June    | $21,000            | $20,500               | ($500)     |
| July    | $22,500            | $20,500               | ($2,000)   |
| August  | $23,500            | $20,500               | ($3,000)   |
| Totals  | $67,000            | $61,500               | ($5,500)   |

Now is a good time to review one of the primary benefits of using the Peace of Mind Schedule—to see possible cash flow problems before they happen. When you are conservative in your projections, the end result is that you have estimated cash balances that are reasonable.

In other words, you are at least 90 percent sure your results will come in at or above the balances projected.

This is a very important point. The last thing you would want to do is have a projection that "muddies the water." By that I mean you would not want a projection that makes it difficult to see a problem lurking under the surface.

You would not want to dive into a body of water without being able to see what lies below the surface. You are much safer when you can see clearly what lies ahead so you can make good decisions.

When the business owner made the revenue projections more conservative, the financial picture changed. With a combined $5,500 reduction in revenues for June through August, the ending cash balance for August changed dramatically. It went from a projected ending balance of $4,000 to a negative balance of $1,500.

Negative cash balances in a projection scream out at you— Problem, Problem, Problem!

What the schedule now told her was that if her cash balance came in at the conservative levels projected, she would run out of cash. She would not have enough money to pay her bills. In particular, she would not have enough cash to make the final balloon payment of $10,000 to her lender.

The most common reaction I get from business owners who have been conservative in their projections, and who have a cash problem staring them in the face like she did, is they instantly want to increase the revenue projection to "get rid of" the problem.

They say, "I have to create higher revenues so I don't run out of cash. I don't have any other choice but to raise the projection."

The better course of action when presented with a problem like this is to do the following:

- Look at the projected cash balance on the schedule that you believe is a problem. Decide what you want that balance to be. Come up with a number that, if you achieve it, will eliminate the problem. In the previous example, the business owner wanted to increase the projected cash balance at the end of August by at least $5,000.
- Write a plan to create the additional cash you need to fix the problem. In the previous example, the plan is a list of action steps to make sure the new marketing plan is a huge success. The business owner's mission was to make sure the actual revenues come in at the more optimistic levels.
- Monitor and tweak the plan each week to make sure it is producing the higher revenues needed.

Your projections will now remain at the conservative levels so you can pass the 90 Percent Test. What changes is that you get even more focused on creating and implementing your plan to arrive at the cash balance you desire.

If the business owner's plan begins to produce at the higher levels (meaning she is actually experiencing the higher revenues), she can consider increasing her projections—but not until then.

The key is to always make sure your projections are conservative. The 90 Percent Test will help you make that happen.

### 4. Use the "Smell Test"

Take a look at the projections again. Look closely at the resulting cash balances. Are they consistent with your general expectations? Are they in line with the actual cash balances over the last six months?

Do they make sense given your intuition and knowledge of the business?

Give the projected cash balances the "smell test." The smell test is a quick way I use to make sure everything smells right. It's a way to check that nothing unusual or unexpected has made its way into your numbers. It is a great way to spot errors. You could have accidentally put a decimal in the wrong place, or entered an extra zero, or made some other data entry error.

It's like picking up a gallon of milk from the refrigerator. It's not a bad idea to give it the quick smell test to make sure you are not about to pour yourself a glass of soured milk. (Better to smell a problem in advance than taste it in the present, right?)

You want to take time to make sure the schedule is error-free and that it passes the smell test. The last thing you want to do to yourself or your business is make business decisions based on faulty projected cash balances.

I once encountered a perfect example that shows why the smell test is so important.

A company was planning a special event and was excited about putting something together that would really dazzle their customers.

After coming up with a rough idea of the kind of event they would like to put on, management realized it would be a good idea to look at the costs associated with the plan.

A schedule of projected costs was quickly thrown together.

The schedule showed something that was a big surprise to everyone. It showed they could add even more bells and whistles to the event because there was plenty of "budget" for it. They ended up throwing an impressive gala. Everyone was proud to be associated with such a class event.

Then the organizers received a rude awakening. It turned out the hastily prepared projection had a big mistake in it. A number had been entered incorrectly. The result of the error was the projected net cost of the event was significantly understated.

The smell test would have caught this mistake.

In fact, when management looked back on it, they all thought it was peculiar that they could put on such a big event for such a small impact on their budget. That was the first sign of a "foul" scent in the air.

The organizers allowed the excitement of putting on the event to cloud their minds. They didn't take the extra time to make sure the end result of the projections made sense.

Don't let this happen to you. Use the smell test to make sure your numbers do not contain something rotten.

## CREATING AND ENTERING YOUR PROJECTIONS

In Chapter 11 we reviewed the process for creating the Peace of Mind Schedule (including how you can get a preformatted Excel file for FREE) and the step-by-step process for entering your last six months of actual cash flow results.

In this chapter we reviewed the four-step process for creating accurate projections.

Now it is time to create and enter your projections for the next six months in the Peace of Mind Schedule.

You will end up with a schedule that has a total of twelve months of cash flows. It will have six months of your actual cash flows and six months of your projected cash flows.

You will then have the answer to the critical cash flow question—What do I expect my cash balance to be six months from now?

For example purposes, let's assume the first six months of actual results you previously entered were January through June. That would make July through December the six months of projections you need to create and enter.

### Section 1—Your Income Statement

Enter the projected revenue and expenses for each of the months July through December. Enter revenues and expenses both as positive numbers.

The schedule will automatically treat expense amounts as deductions from EBITDA and the cash balance. If you are creating the schedule yourself, set the formulas up so the expense items in this section are treated as deductions from cash flow.

## Section 2—Cash You Use for Debt Service

Enter your projected debt service payments for each month.

These are the payments you make on loans with your bank or other financial institution or person who has loaned you money. The amount you enter here needs to be the total payments. This includes both principal and interest for the total of all payments made on loans or other debt.

Enter payments in this section as a negative number. If you expect to borrow any money during the period, you would enter that as a positive number.

## Section 3—Cash You Invest in the Business

Enter the projected cash outlays that represent investments in your business.

The most common item in this section is capital expenditures. This is cash you project to spend for assets that must be capitalized (recorded on the balance sheet rather than expensed when purchased).

Enter these amounts as a negative number. If you expect to sell an asset during the period, you would enter the proceeds as a positive number.

## Section 4—Other Cash Flow Items

This section of the schedule is primarily focused on capturing the various "timing differences" created in your income statement by the accrual basis of accounting.

We discussed earlier how the accrual basis of accounting requires certain revenues and expenses to be recognized in a month different from when the actual money is received or paid out. Those "timing differences" are taken into account here in order to show the actual impact your results had on your cash balance.

Use the last six months of actual results in the schedule as a guide as you project each of these amounts.

## Your Action Plan

✔ Take time to look back at the four-step process for creating accurate projections. These steps will help ensure that your projections are realistic and useful.

✔ Use the 90 Percent Test to make sure your projections are conservative.

✔ Use the "smell test" to make sure your projections make sense and are free from errors or mistakes. This will save you from making decisions based on inaccurate information.

## Send Me Your Questions

If you have any questions, concerns, or comments, please feel free to send them to me at pcampbell@growandsucceed.com. I respond to all my e-mail personally and promptly.

# Chapter 13

## Key Insights About Your Cash Flow

*Decide what you want, decide what you are willing to exchange for it.*
*Establish your priorities and go to work.*
—H. L. HUNT, AMERICAN OIL MAGNATE

Now you have the Peace of Mind schedule set up, your last six months of actual cash flow results are entered and verified, and you have the next six months of projected cash flow results entered. You have the information you need now to understand what's going on with the cash flow of your business.

The next step is to review the schedule to see what it has revealed to you about your cash flow. When I walk through this review process, I like to make a list of "learnings" or "key insights" as I go through each step. Making a list like this will come in handy when it is time to create your action plan for how you will better manage your cash flow and how you plan to make your business even better in the future.

Below is a seven-step review that will help ensure you get the maximum benefit from the schedule. The steps focus primarily on reviewing sections 3, 4, and 5 of your completed Peace of Mind schedule.

## 1. Understand the Peak and Trough Cash Months

The peak cash month is that month (or months) where your cash balance is generally at its highest point during the year. The trough cash month is just the opposite. It is the month (or months) where your cash balance is generally at its lowest point during the year.

Almost every business will have a month or a portion of the year where their cash balances are generally the highest. They will also have a particular month or period during the year where their cash balance will be at its lowest levels during the year. This happens in businesses where sales or expenses (or both) are not evenly spread throughout the year. An extreme example would be a store that sells Christmas ornaments and decorations. Sales would be very slow during the summer and very high in the months leading up to Christmas. As a result, their cash balances would be highest during the peak selling season and lowest during the summer.

I worked with a company whose peak cash month was January and the trough cash month was October. The difference between the peak balance and the trough balance was about $800,000. Their minimum cash target was $150,000. That meant the peak cash balance in January had to be at least $950,000 in order for them to have a trough cash balance of at least $150,000 in October.

The Peace of Mind schedule showed them exactly where the cash balance should be at the peak and trough months. This provided them the information they needed to manage the business properly and to protect the trough month. It made it crystal clear how the seasonality of their business affected their cash flow each month of the year. And most importantly, it made it clear that they could not just spend the money they had sitting there in January.

This is where many business owners make a big mistake with their cash flow. When they are in their peak cash month, they feel really good about their cash flow because they have a nice cash balance. Then they make decisions that use or commit that money not realizing that they are using cash they will need in order to get them through the trough month.

The result is a "cash flow problem" when the inevitable trough month arrives and there is not enough cash to get through that period. Without the schedule to define the peak and the trough periods precisely, they are basically flying blind. They can only hope and pray everything will turn out all right.

In my opinion, this is one of the major killers of small businesses today. The tendency to use or commit cash when the cash balance looks good is a very strong one. The cure is to understand your peak and trough periods. Look at the schedule to see when your peak and trough months are. Then always keep this concept in mind so you can manage your business and your cash flow according to that understanding.

## 2. Review Your Debt Service Obligations

If you have a fixed monthly payment you make on a loan or other obligation, then the debt service section of the schedule will not vary much each month. On the other hand, if you have a balloon payment you make from time to time or you are required to pay down on a revolving line of credit, you need to make sure this section properly reflects those obligations.

The schedule is especially helpful when you make debt service payments that are bigger in some months than in others. Setting out your obligations here will help you make sure you have enough cash to meet those commitments.

This is also an area of the schedule to look to if you expect to have (or are having) a cash flow problem. One of your options to fix the problem is to consider restructuring your debt service obligations. If you can present a well thought out plan to your lending institution, you may be able to re-schedule your existing payment obligations in order to help you fix the cash flow problem.

Showing them the Peace of Mind schedule will greatly improve your chances here because they will appreciate the fact that you have a good grasp of what's going on with your cash flow. They will instantly recognize that you are in control of the cash. And that will increase your odds of getting their approval for a revised payment arrangement.

### 3. Pay Special Attention to Capital Expenditures

Capital expenditures is a category that can surprise you unless you actively manage and control it each month. A capital expenditure is recorded on your balance sheet rather than as an expense in your income statement. The cost of the asset you purchased is then depreciated over the life of the asset. As a result, you don't see the cost of that expenditure show up immediately in your income statement. It's this accounting treatment for capital expenditures that makes it so important that you manage it closely.

I worked with a company once that learned this lesson the hard way. They were getting close to the end of their annual budgeting process. The budget was very tight and the President was forcing his vice presidents to reduce their budgeted expenses even further. Each person was looking very closely at every $500–$1,000 expense in their budget. They were trying to cut enough of those relatively small expenditures to get down to the overall budgeted expense levels set by the President.

They did in fact cut a number of those expenses out of the budget. They also did a good job during the year of keeping the actual expenses in line with the budget. The big surprise came at the end of the year when the President realized that capital expenditures had more than doubled during the year. Capital expenditures totaled almost $200,000 for the year compared to less than $100,000 the previous year.

What happened? Management was so focused on the income statement and keeping expenses down that they let over $100,000 leak out of the company through the "back door." There was no capital expenditures budget. There was also no schedule in place to see how much money was being spent each month on items that were recorded on the balance sheet rather than recognized as an expense in the income statement when incurred.

Once the Peace of Mind schedule was set up and completed, the President saw what had happened during the year. Reviewing this part of the schedule helped him to see why the schedule was so valuable as a tool to manage his cash flow. It also reinforced for him the fact that the basic financial statements alone are insufficient to properly manage the cash flow of a business.

Pay special attention to your capital expenditures so you don't end up with a similar surprise.

## 4. A Sale Is Not Complete Until the Cash Is Collected

The first two lines in section 4 are focused on the difference between your sales as reported in the income statement and the dollar value of the cash you actually collected, or received that month. You will have a difference here if the product or service you sell is not paid for by your customer at the same time you sell it. If you invoice your customer at the time of sale, then the timing of your actual cash receipts is determined by when you collect the amount you invoiced the customer.

Business owners are often surprised to see that their cash collected number is not always consistent with their sales. This provides a wake-up call. Making the sale is very important. But collecting the money for the sale is also extremely important. It does not do any good to sell a product if you don't collect your money. In fact, you can ruin a business real fast if you neglect the all-important step of making sure you are collecting the money for what you sell.

I had the President of a national association of small business owners tell me a story about one of their members that really highlights this point. One of their members started a service business catering to large health care institutions. She would provide a trained staff of people to perform services that the institution would otherwise have to hire employees to perform. She provided a turnkey service that would help improve the service levels while at the same time save the institution money.

After she got her first contract, she began the process of recruiting, interviewing, hiring, creating an extensive training program, training the new hires, etc. This took about three months to complete. After her team was in place and trained, they began providing the service. She sent her invoice to the institution after the first month of services had been provided. After a couple months went by she got a really big surprise.

It turns out this institution held invoices from suppliers for at least 120 days before they paid them. In fact, it was somewhat of an industry practice. She was now almost seven months into her new business and she had not even collected the first dollar of revenue. She had been spending money all this time not realizing there would be this huge delay in actually collecting her money.

Unfortunately, she ran out of cash. When she started the business she thought she would be able to get everything going faster and she thought she would be able to do it a little cheaper. But the really big surprise came when she realized the hard way that creating a sale and collecting the cash doesn't always happen at the same time.

Another benefit of this part of the schedule is to help reduce bad debt expense. Most businesses that invoice their customers and get paid after they make the sale do not collect 100% of their accounts receivable. The amount they do not collect is considered a bad debt expense.

If your business is in this category, you need to closely manage your accounts receivable collections relative to your sales. Having your sales and the cash you collect during the month right next to each other makes it very easy to manage and control. If you see that the amount collected during a month is falling off, you can quickly get to the heart of the issue and get your collections back on track.

I saw how critical this was with a business that had inadvertently allowed its bad debt expense to climb significantly. It happened as a result of a falloff in the speed with which they collected their accounts receivable. Unfortunately, the company did not see the falloff until it was well into its third year of decline. This ended up costing them a lot of money.

Review your actual and projected sales and cash collected in section 4 to see what it reveals to you about your cash flow. Look to see if you need to make a note of any key insights here that you can take action on once your review of the Peace of Mind schedule is complete.

## 5. Inventory Can Hurt You Real Fast

The third and fourth lines in section 4 show your cost of goods sold together with your inventory purchases. The accounting for inventory makes it very important that you manage this cash outlay very carefully. When you buy inventory, the transaction is recorded as an addition to inventory on your balance sheet. The expense for that inventory item is not recorded as an expense in the income statement until the item is sold.

It's the timing of the recording of the expense that makes inventory such a unique animal. While you are writing the checks, the cash is leaving your bank account but there is no recognition of that item as an expense. This section of the Peace of Mind schedule will help you keep a close eye on how much inventory you are buying compared to how much you are selling.

This area is one that is especially critical for a retail business. I worked with a retail operation recently that had let their inventory get a bit out of control. The owner did a good job of reviewing the income statement each month. What he had not done quite as well was reviewing the amount of cash his stores were using each month to purchase inventory.

The operation was short on cash and the owner was concerned that he had a problem. He was right. It turned out the stores had about twice as much inventory on the books as they should have. They had been buying more inventory than they were selling. Some of the inventory had been moved to storage locations because there was not enough room for it in the stores. It had become clear that they had not managed their inventory purchases properly.

The product had to be marked down 60–80 percent in order to sell it and clear out the excess inventory. The good news was they were able to generate some cash. The bad news was they had to do it at a big loss. And it was only at this point that the reality of this loss was shown in the income statement. That's part of inventory's ability to hurt you real fast.

The best medicine here is prevention. Review your actual and projected inventory purchases relative to your cost of goods sold to see what it reveals to you about your cash flow. Look to see if you need to make a note of any key insights here that you can take action on once your review of the Peace of Mind schedule is complete. This will help you stay in control and make sure your inventory buying is disciplined and focused.

## 6. Paying Your Taxes Requires Good Planning (and Thinking Inside the Box)

This line shows the estimated income taxes you are paying each month or each quarter. In many small businesses you really don't know what your actual tax expense will be until you get to the end of the year. As a result, the tax expense is oftentimes not recorded in your income statement until after the end of the year. This line in the schedule shows the amount of cash you are paying, and will be paying, toward the your income taxes for the year even though that expense may not be recorded yet in your income statement.

I saw a great cartoon strip in the *Wall Street Journal* that did an incredible job of portraying my advice to you with regard to how you manage and pay your taxes. The comic showed a picture of two businessmen in jail. They were both behind bars sitting on a bench. One of the men was looking a bit contemplative and said to the other "Let's just say, with accounting, it's best to think inside the box."

116

This cartoon was being shown at a time when the business headlines were filled with stories about companies whose financial statements turned out to be less than accurate. Where there was some "cooking of the books" and some reporting of financial results that was intended to mislead those who were reading the financial statements.

The cartoon was making the point that accounting is not one of those areas where you have to be a creative genius. Accounting is about recording and reporting transactions as they actually happen. There is no need to be inventive or attempt to push the bounds of legitimacy. There is definitely no reason to attempt to re-write the rules or find out how far you can bend the rules. The best approach is to record the facts as they happen then present the financial statements based on those facts.

This approach also sums up my advice with regard to your taxes. It's not a good idea to be too creative or inventive when it comes to paying your taxes. You are much better off to play it safe and operate in accordance with the rules. You want to have a good CPA or tax advisor so that you can do some effective tax planning and make sure that if something can be deducted that it is. The key though is to color inside the lines, stay within the rules, because it is not wise to push the boundaries of the tax laws.

Review this line of the schedule carefully with your CPA or tax advisor to make sure you have a good estimate of your taxes for the year and then make sure that those estimates are getting paid each month or each quarter. That way you will not end up with any negative surprises when you file your tax return.

### 7. Watch Accounts Payable Closely

This line in section 4 is the change in your accounts payable balance each month. It's simply a calculation right off your balance sheet. You should watch this line closely to make sure the amount of the change is relatively small each month.

117

One of the things you want to watch out for is that you are not improving your cash flow by not paying your bills as they become due. When this number is positive, it means you have expenses that have been recorded but the invoice has not yet been paid. This will certainly happen in some months. The key here is to make sure that, over time, you are paying your bills as they become due. This will keep your accounts payable balance from growing.

### Action Steps to Improve My Business and My Cash Flow

Now it's time to take the insights and learnings from your in-depth review of your Peace of Mind schedule and put your "next steps" in writing. What specific steps do you need to take now that you have reviewed your cash flow? As you reviewed the schedule, did you make note of some areas where you want to make changes or improvements?

Take a few minutes to write down your next steps so you can put these key insights to work in your business.

1. How I will manage my business so I always protect my trough cash month (the period during the year where my cash balance is the lowest).

   _____

   _____

   _____


2. How I will manage my debt service obligations and not over-extend myself.

   _____

   _____

   _____

3. How I will manage my capital expenditures so I always know exactly how much cash flow is being devoted to re-investing in my business.

   _____

   _____

   _____

4. How I will manage my sales and accounts receivable to make sure I am collecting the money due to me.

   _____

   _____

   _____

5. How I will manage my inventory to make sure my buying is disciplined and focused.

   _____

   _____

   _____

6. How I will manage my taxes so I don't have any negative surprises at the end of the year.

   _____

   _____

   _____

7. How I will manage my accounts payable so I pay all my obligations on or before the due date.

   _____

   _____

   _____

8. Other areas of my business and my cash flow I will work each day to improve.

   _____

   _____

   _____

# Your Action Plan

- ✔ Once you have created the Peace of Mind schedule, follow the step-by-step process to ensure you get the maximum benefit from the schedule.

- ✔ Understand your peak and trough cash months. Make sure that every business decision you make is done in the context of its expected impact on your trough cash balance.

- ✔ A sale is not complete until the cash is collected. Remember that regardless of whether a sale has been reflected in your income statement, what ultimately matters is that you collect the cash.

- ✔ Inventory can hurt you real fast. If inventory is a component of your business, it is extremely important that you clearly understand how it is accounted for in your financial statements (especially the income statement). You need to make sure your buying is disciplined and focused so it does not come back to haunt you in the future.

## Send Me Your Questions

If you have any questions, concerns, or comments, please feel free to send them to me at pcampbell@growandsucceed.com. I respond to all my e-mail personally and promptly.

# Chapter 14

## Creating Peace of Mind Each Month

*Great works are performed not by strength, but by perseverance.*
—SAMUEL JOHNSON, AUTHOR

Maintaining the Peace of Mind schedule each month is an easy process. In fact, I'm almost positive that you will actually enjoy the process. Why? Because it provides such valuable information about your most precious asset—Your CASH.

Knowing you have your cash flow under control is a wonderful feeling. Updating the schedule each month is how you ensure that you always maintain that control.

The Peace of Mind Schedule will become an important tool in your business tool kit. You will find it to be a helpful resource to consult before making important business decisions.

It's important to point out that the principles we have discussed so far apply to all businesses regardless of their size. The Peace of Mind schedule looks basically the same whether you have a very small home-based business you run on the side or whether you own or manage a multi-billion dollar global enterprise.

The beauty of the schedule lies in the simple and clear way in which it reveals to you what's really going on with the cash flow of your business. It reveals the same insights regardless of the size of the business using it.

Here is an example to show you what I mean. The schedule below is a portion of the Peace of Mind schedule we looked at in Chapter 11.

**Cash Is King, Inc.**
**The Peace of Mind Schedule**
**Year:** _____

|                        | January   |
|------------------------|-----------|
| Beginning cash balance | $10,000   |
| **Section 1**          |           |
| Revenues               |           |
| Sales                  | 15,000    |
| Other                  | 0         |
| Total                  | 15,000    |
| Cost of goods sold     | 3,750     |
| Gross profit           | $11,250   |

This a portion of the schedule for a small specialty retail store. It shows sales in January of $15,000 and a gross profit of $11,250.

Now let's look at the same schedule with one "slight" modification.

**Cash Is King, Inc.**
**The Peace of Mind Schedule**
**Year:** _____
(amounts shown are in thousands)

|                        | January   |
|------------------------|-----------|
| Beginning cash balance | $10,000   |
| **Section 1**          |           |
| Revenues               |           |
| Sales                  | 15,000    |
| Other                  | 0         |
| Total                  | 15,000    |
| Cost of goods sold     | 3,750     |
| Gross profit           | $11,250   |

The "slight" change is that the schedule now includes a statement on it that says—"(amounts shown are in thousands)."

Now the schedule shows January sales of $15 million ($15,000,000) and a gross profit of $11.25 million ($11,250,000). This business is very different in size to the business in the previous example. This retail business is one with hundreds of stores. It is a much larger business than the single specialty retail store.

But there is no difference in how the Peace of Mind schedule works. There is no difference in how the schedule is set up and maintained each month. There is no difference in the value that it provides to you as a business owner or manager.

So don't let yourself fall into the trap of thinking your business is either too small or too large to benefit from the schedule. The schedule provides you the insight you need to manage your business properly regardless of the size of the business.

## FOUR STEPS TO MAINTAINING THE PEACE OF MIND SCHEDULE

### 1. Enter Your Most Recent Actual Results

You always want to enter each month's actual results as soon as you have them. You want to do this to make sure you have the most up-to-date cash balance possible.

Remember, the schedule always shows a "rolling cash balance." So if you had a projected ending cash balance for July of $6,000 and it actually came in at $5,000, every month after July would also be overstated by $1,000 (the $6,000 projected balance less the $5,000 actual balance).

You want to get your actual results in as quickly as possible so your projected cash balances are based on accurate beginning balances.

### 2. Compare Your Actual Cash Flow Results to Your Projected Results

This step is the secret to making your projections better as well as easier to update each month. It also helps you better understand the financial implications of the way you manage your business.

Let's say you just entered your actual cash flow results for July. Take a look at the ending cash balance to see how it compares to the ending cash balance you had projected (I always print a copy of the schedule and file it just before I update a particular month).

You want to see how well you projected your cash flow for the month. If you missed it by a large amount, then look through each line of your actual results and your projections to see where you made your error. Did an unusual event happen that month? Did you neglect to take something into account when you made the projection originally?

This process of comparing your actual results to your projections will do more to help you understand your business than almost anything else you could do.

### 3. Make Any Necessary Modifications to Your Projections

Now that you have entered your actual results for the most recent month and compared it to your projection, use what you learned in that exercise to make your projections even better. Are sales trending above your original projections? Are sales trending below your expectations?

Take a look at your cash flow projections for the next six months. Are you still comfortable that they meet the 90 Percent Test? Are they conservative?

This is also a good time to give your projections the "smell test" to make sure there are no errors or mistakes in the numbers.

Consider anything in the business that has changed that will have an influence on your cash flow. Make any tweaks or changes necessary.

This process will help you get better at projecting your cash flow. And the better your projections, the better prepared you are to make more enlightened and profitable business decisions.

## 4. Determine Any Action Steps to Change the Cash Balance

The Peace of Mind Schedule is up-to-date and your projections have been reviewed and updated. The schedule shows clearly what your cash balance is and what you expect it to be in six months.

Now you want to look at those projected cash balances to see if you are happy with them. Are the balances consistent with your financial goals for the business?

If the answer is yes, then it's time to put the schedule away and focus on the steps you have to take each day to create the results you have projected.

If the answer is no, then you have some more work to do.

You have to determine how big the problem is, when it might happen, and then make your plan to fix the problem. In Chapter 7 we talked about the fact that to know you have a possible cash flow problem is not enough information to get you to a solution.

You have to know how much of a problem you have and when it will be a problem. You have to put a dollar amount and a time-frame on the problem.

Here is an example we looked at in Chapter 7. Which of the following statements will help move you to a solution?

- I'm concerned I may be short of cash sometime soon!
  Or
- I expect to be $5,000 short of cash at the end of April.

Neither statement is good news. However, the second statement gives you the information you need to do something about the problem. You know how much you expect the problem to be and when it is likely to become a reality.

Now you can make a list of all the ways you can increase revenues, reduce expenses, reduce capital expenditures, restructure debt obligations, and so on. This helps you focus on creating a specific plan so you can take action, and that's really the key to making sure the problem does not actually happen.

Have a goal clearly in mind, create a specific plan to achieve the goal, implement the plan, then measure your progress against the plan. That's how you dramatically increase the likelihood that you create the cash flow results you deserve from your business.

# Your Action Plan

✔ Make a commitment to yourself that you will use the Peace of Mind Schedule every month.

✔ Make sure you take the time each month to compare your actual cash flow results to your projected cash flow results. This is the secret to making your projections better each month.

✔ When your projections indicate you may end up with a cash balance you don't like, take action. Make a list of all the ways you can increase revenues, reduce costs, reduce capital expenditures, or restructure debt. Then, work single-mindedly on that list.

# Send Me Your Questions

If you have any questions, concerns, or comments, please feel free to send them to me at pcampbell@growandsucceed.com. I respond to all my e-mail personally and promptly.

# Chapter 15

## A Real World Example

*Take the attitude of a student, never be too big to ask questions, never know too much to learn something new.*
—OG MANDINO, AUTHOR AND SPEAKER

I would like to bring the process of taking control of your cash flow together for you in an example that is very typical in business today. This example is a sort of mini-case study to help you see how the principles you have learned so far are applied. It also demonstrates the amazing insights you can learn about your business and your cash flow.

I have taken several experiences I have had with business owners and combined them into this example. That way you get the benefit of these very important insights that come from learning what other business owners have done to regain control of their business and their cash flow.

We will look at an example of a business before the owner discovered the two critical cash flow questions. You will see the concerns and frustrations he felt trying to manage the business. We will look at the dilemma he faced and how the step-by-step process for taking control of his cash flow made all the difference.

He came to some very important realizations as he saw the business from an entirely new perspective. In fact, some of those realizations began to surface even before we had completed the Peace of Mind schedule. The process brought new information to his attention in a way he had never experienced before.

He went from being worried and concerned about his cash flow to knowing exactly what he needed to do to make the business instantly better. Not to mention the fact that he learned how to make sure he always had the cash flow of his business under control.

## LEARNING FROM OTHER BUSINESS OWNERS

One of the hallmarks of a successful business owner is a willingness to learn from *other* successful business owners. They are always talking to other business owners to get ideas they can put to work in their own business. They share what has worked for them and learn what has worked for others.

In his book *Focal Point,* Brian Tracy said this about the tremendous impact this principle had on his life and his career.

> "The turning point in my life came when I discovered the law of cause and effect, the great law of the universe and human destiny. I learned that everything happens for a reason. I discovered that success is not an accident. Failure is not an accident, either.
>
> I also discovered that people who are successful in any area usually are those who have learned the cause-and-effect relationship between what they want and how to get it. They then did repeatedly what other successful people did in a particular area until they got the same results. This insight changed my life."
>
> —*Brian Tracy, Focal Point*

In the case of your cash flow, the "cause" is the action you take to regain control of your cash flow. The "effect" is the positive result that naturally flows from knowing what's going on with your cash flow. You experience the insights that will help you make more intelligent and profitable business decisions.

It all starts when you implement the step-by-step process like the owner did in the example we are about to look at. As you read the example, remember how important it is to learn from others. Remember that your success in business will be determined in large part by your commitment to take action. Use the lessons you will learn in this example and make sure you follow the same steps.

Also, keep in mind that the principles and insights you will discover in this example apply to all businesses regardless of their size. The example we will look at here is a single store example, but the same lessons would apply if this were a chain of hundreds or thousands of stores. The step-by-step process for taking control of your cash flow is basically the same regardless of how big or how small your business is.

## SUMMARY OF THE BUSINESS

The business we will look at in our example is a specialty retail store. The owner runs the store and devotes full-time to making it a success. Like many small business owners, he wears many hats. He is in charge of Marketing, Operations, Customer Service, Finance, Administration, Human Resources, and everything else that must be done to run a successful business.

He has a bookkeeper who handles the day-to-day accounting functions. The bookkeeper gets the bills paid, creates the financial statements each month, reconciles the bank statements, and all the other functions related to accounting for the store.

Here is a brief summary of the business:

- The store sells home furnishings like tables, lamps, framed art, decorative accessories, and other interior accent pieces for the home. They have a great reputation in the community for providing a unique product style and mix. The owner is a very good merchant and customers notice it as soon as they walk in the store. The store displays a product offering that is much more exciting and unique than any of the competitors.

- The store did just under $520,000 in sales last year. Income before taxes last year was about $105,000. Sales so far this year (January through September) are up about 14 percent and income before taxes are up about 26 percent. The store operates on a calendar year basis. As a result, financial statements and tax returns are prepared using January as the first month of the year and December as the end of the year.

- The store is in a nice lifestyle retail center in an affluent part of town. The center attracts customers from a wide area and from some of the best neighborhoods in the city. The store normally experiences much higher customer traffic and sales during the last two months of the year. This is partly a result of customers buying gifts for other people and partly because management of the center does a very good job of marketing and promoting the center around the holiday season. November and December make up about 29 percent of sales for the year.

Despite the success of the business and the nice increase in sales and income before taxes, the owner was becoming nervous. He was short of cash and having trouble paying his bills on time. He was frustrated, confused, and most of all he was embarrassed because he could not pay all the bills that were due. He was forced to come up with excuses he could tell his vendors about why he needed more time to pay their invoices.

Of course, the vendors were also becoming concerned. They were a bit surprised that he could run such a seemingly successful business and yet not be able to pay their invoices on time.

# UNDERSTANDING THE CASH FLOW WORRIES

Knowing an owner is worried about cash flow, I don't go immediately to asking the two critical cash flow questions. Instead, I first ask the owner to describe for me the things he or she is worried about. I ask the owner to describe the problems, concerns, and frustrations they are experiencing regarding their cash flow.

This provides me a good idea of where their real problem lies. It's amazing how fast you can see what's going on in a business when owners share their most pressing problems and concerns. It helps shed some light on the relatively small number of "core problems" that are causing the majority of the "undesirable effects" they are living with in their business.

My experience has been that, in most businesses, a relatively small number of problems create most of the frustrations, complications, and concerns that fill a person's mind each day. This process of having business owners tell me all the problems they are experiencing helps me get to the two or three issues that are creating the majority of the most nagging and difficult problems.

Oftentimes an owner will list the most difficult problems and frustrations. After we go through the process of answering the two critical cash flow questions, I can show them that there were only one or two issues (the core problems) that were creating all of the problems and frustrations (the undesirable effects).

Here is a summary of the problems, concerns, and frustrations in our retail store example:

- The owner was uncomfortable because he couldn't pay all his bills. Vendors were becoming irritated and had even threatened to start holding his orders if he did not take care of the past due invoices quickly.

- This same cash flow crunch happened last year about the same time. In August and September, he is ordering the merchandise that he will need to have in the store during the seasonally strong selling months of November and December. Just when he needs his vendors the most seems to be the time it is most difficult to pay the invoices on time. The fact that it is happening again this year is putting an even bigger strain on his relationship with his most important merchandise vendors.

- He was hearing a complaint from customers that he was sometimes out of stock on items they wanted to buy. Because of the 30 to 45 day lead times for ordering and receiving merchandise, he could not always convince the customer to place the order and wait for delivery. He knew he was missing out on thousands of dollars of sales as a result. Even worse, he knew he was missing a golden opportunity to grow his list of satisfied customers.

- He is making more money than ever before—at least that's what the financial statements are saying. On the one hand, he feels like he must be doing something right because the financial statements show that he is continuing to make more money each year. On the other hand, he feels like something must be wrong because he should have more cash on hand to pay his bills and grow the business.

- He is concerned that he will have to reduce the amount of money he takes out of the business for himself each year in order to help solve the cash flow problem. In fact, he had to forgo his normal monthly distribution from the business beginning in August because of his cash flow problems.

- He has always wanted to open a second location on the opposite side of town. There is a big market that his current location is not serving. He is worried that he will never be able to expand the business if he is having a hard time making ends meet with only one store.

**The Two Critical Cash Flow Questions**

Having listed the primary problems and concerns, it was time to answer the two questions that instantly tell you whether you have the cash flow of your business under control.

### 1. What is my cash balance right now?

In our example, the owner had the answer to this question at his fingertips. The bookkeeper did a very good job of doing today's work today. She entered the cash receipts shortly after the end of each day. She processed invoices as she received them and got them into the accounting system quickly. And she reconciled the cash balance to the bank balance within just a couple days of receiving the bank statement.

### 2. What do I expect my cash balance to be six months from now?

The owner did not have the answer to this question. This is the case with the overwhelming majority of business owners today. The cash flow survey we looked at in Chapter 1 showed that only 21 percent of the business owners in the survey could answer this question.

Since the Peace of Mind schedule is the tool for answering this question, we moved directly into getting the schedule set up and prepared. The owner had considered Cash Flow Rule #5—Either you do the work or have someone else do it. He realized his time was much better spent making sure all the pieces of the puzzle were in place for the upcoming selling season.

My job then was to complete the schedule and bring him the results. We would then review what the Peace of Mind schedule revealed about exactly what was going on with his cash flow.

## CREATING THE PEACE OF MIND SCHEDULE

The step-by-step process for completing the Peace of Mind schedule is set out in Chapters 11 and 12. Chapter 11 sets out how to set up the schedule and enter the last six months of actual results in the schedule. Chapter 12 sets out how to create and enter the projected results for the next six months.

We followed the process set out in these two chapters to set up the schedule. Below is a summary of the step-by-step process we followed.

1. **Set Up the Spreadsheet.** We used the same Peace of Mind schedule you can download for FREE at www.neverrunoutofcash.com/freetools.htm. It is a pre-formatted Excel spreadsheet that is set up and ready for you to use.

2. **Make Changes to Track Your Income Statement.** The Peace of Mind schedule comes with some generic revenue and expense categories set up in section 1. These had to be changed so they tracked the income statement categories in the store's financial statements. I got a copy of the income statement format and changed the revenue and expense categories in section 1 of the schedule to match that format.

3. **Enter the Previous Six Months of Cash Flow Data.** The first step here was to get copies of the financial statements of the store that we could use to enter the actual results. Here is a list of the financial statements we gathered for this process.

**Income statement**

- Results for each month of the current year. In this case, it was the months of January through September.
- Year-to-date results for the current year and for the same period in the prior year.
- Full year results for the prior year.

**Balance Sheet**

- Each month of the current year.
- December of the prior year.

The year-to-date and prior year income statements are summarized in Exhibit 2. The balance sheets for the most recent month and the end of the prior year are summarized in Exhibit 3. Take a minute to review these financial statements so you can see the financial results our business owner had been looking at.

Now let's walk through each section of the Peace of Mind schedule to see what we did to enter the actual results into the schedule. Each step below is set out in the same order as the instructions are presented in Chapter 11. We first entered the month of January by following the step-by-step instructions. After the first month is complete and the numbers are accurate, we go to the next step and enter the remaining months of actual results.

## Section 1—The Income Statement

We entered the first month's revenues and expenses. This is a very straightforward process because we had already modified the revenue and expense categories to track the format of the store's income statement.

After entering the numbers for the month, we verified that the revenue and expense amounts were entered correctly.

## Section 2—Cash Used for Debt Service

We entered the total debt service payments made during the month on the store's bank loan. The amount entered here includes both principal and interest. This is the total of all payments each month related to the debt the store is obligated to pay.

We got this number from the check register recap in the store's accounting system.

## Section 3—Cash Invested in the Business

We entered the capital expenditures made during the month. The owner had purchased a pre-owned van for cash in January. He planned to use it for customer deliveries. The van must be recorded

**Exhibit 2**

**The Home Furnishings Store**

**Income Statement**

| | Jan–Sep Current Year | Jan–Sep Prior Year | Full 12 Months Prior Year |
|---|---|---|---|
| Revenues | | | |
| Sales | $382,700 | $337,042 | $519,324 |
| Other | 1,476 | 1,476 | 1,968 |
| Total | 384,176 | 338,518 | 521,292 |
| Cost of goods sold | 188,559 | 162,450 | 247,671 |
| Gross profit | 195,617 | 176,068 | 273,621 |
| Operating expenses | | | |
| Employee wages and taxes | 45,835 | 44,072 | 60,333 |
| Rent | 42,743 | 42,158 | 56,210 |
| Advertising and marketing | 11,481 | 10,111 | 15,580 |
| Insurance | 2,096 | 1,923 | 1,923 |
| Repairs and maintenance | 350 | 285 | 331 |
| Telephone and utilities | 8,339 | 8,065 | 11,394 |
| Travel, meals, and entertainment | 1,543 | 1,446 | 1,684 |
| Credit card and bank fees | 4,592 | 4,044 | 6,232 |
| Legal and accounting | 2,335 | 2,238 | 2,616 |
| Office supplies and expenses | 315 | 180 | 240 |
| Dues and subscriptions | 225 | 90 | 120 |
| Depreciation & amortization | 6,727 | 5,522 | 7,362 |
| Miscellaneous | 548 | 560 | 710 |
| Total | 127,129 | 120,694 | 164,735 |
| Operating income | 68,488 | 55,374 | 108,886 |
| Interest | 2,515 | 3,086 | 4,021 |
| Miscellaneous | 55 | 33 | 47 |
| Total | 2,570 | 3,119 | 4,068 |
| Pretax income | $ 65,918 | $ 52,255 | $104,818 |

**Exhibit 3**

**The Home Furnishings Store**

**Balance Sheet**

| ASSETS | September of the Current Year | December of the Prior Year |
|---|---|---|
| **Current Assets** | | |
| Cash | $2,480 | $42,880 |
| Accounts receivable | 18,120 | 0 |
| Inventory | 89,758 | 61,959 |
| Other current assets | 6,369 | 6,250 |
| Total current assets | 116,727 | 111,089 |
| **Property** | | |
| Leasehold improvements | 43,180 | 43,180 |
| Furniture, fixtures, and equipment | 32,560 | 21,310 |
| Gross property | 75,740 | 64,490 |
| Less accumulated depreciation | (36,176) | (29,449) |
| Net property | 39,564 | 35,041 |
| Total Assets | $156,291 | $146,130 |
| **LIABILITIES & EQUITY** | | |
| **Current Liabilities** | | |
| Accounts payable & accrued liabilities | $24,113 | $23,411 |
| Current portion of notes payable | 11,997 | 11,385 |
| Total current liabilities | 36,110 | 34,796 |
| **Long-Term Debt** | | |
| Notes payable | 31,173 | 40,249 |
| **Equity** | | |
| Owner's investment | 30,000 | 30,000 |
| Retained earnings | 59,008 | 41,085 |
| Total equity | 89,008 | 71,085 |
| Total Liabilities and Equity | $156,291 | $146,130 |

as an asset of the business rather than expensed in the income statement when it was purchased.

## Section 4—Other Cash Flow Items

Completing this part of the schedule begins to really shed some light on the actual cash flow of the business. Let's look at how we handled each line in this section of the schedule.

*Deduct: sales*—this line is a formula in the schedule that takes sales from section 1 and deducts it here.

*Add: cash collected from sales and accounts receivable*—we entered the cash collected during the month for sales made that month and for cash that was collected on accounts receivable. This gives us the amount of cash collected regardless of what month the related sale was made.

*Add: cost of goods sold*—this line is a formula in the schedule that takes the cost of goods sold from section 1 and adds it back to cash flow. We do that because not all of the cost of goods sold expense line represents cash that was actually paid out during the month.

*Deduct: inventory purchases*—we entered the amount of cash actually used to purchase inventory during the month. The previous line added back the cost of goods sold expense from the income statement. We do that because the cost of an item sold in a month is recorded as an expense in the same month it was sold, regardless of when the inventory item was actually purchased.

The inventory purchases line allows us to see how much cash we actually used to purchase inventory, regardless of whether we sold the product that month or not.

*Estimated tax payments*—we entered the estimated tax payments that were sent to the Internal Revenue Service.

*Change in accounts payable*—we entered the change in accounts payable for the month. This is a quick way to adjust for the effect the accrual basis of accounting has on the recording of expenses in the income statement.

*Other*—this line is for entering any miscellaneous items or cash flow timing differences not specifically captured in a separate line in section 4. This line should usually be a fairly small number and should not vary much from month to month.

*Net cash flow*—this line is a formula in the schedule that calculates the net cash flow for the month.

*Ending cash balance*—this line takes the beginning cash balance for the month and adds or subtracts the net cash flow for the month. We made sure that this line was equal to the cash balance on the balance sheet for that month. This way we know the data we just entered is accurate.

*Minimum cash balance target*—this line serves as a reminder that you need to have a certain minimum cash balance at the end of each month. We set this line to $15,000. Any balance below that number would be cause for alarm.

## Entering the Most Recent Six Months of Actual Cash Flows

With the first month entered in the schedule, we followed the same step-by-step process to enter the other months. We decided to go ahead and enter the months of January through September so we would have each month of the current year in front of us. That would provide us the information we would need to see exactly what was going on with the store's cash flow.

Exhibit 4 shows the Peace of Mind schedule as it looked after we had completed the loading of actual results for January through September.

## Creating and Entering the Cash Flow Projections

Now it was time to complete the schedule by creating the cash flow projections for the next six months (October through March). This will provide us the information to answer the second of the two critical cash

# Exhibit 4

## The Home Furnishings Store
## The Peace of Mind Schedule
### January–September of the Current Year

| | Actual Jan | Actual Feb | Actual Mar | Actual Apr | Actual May | Actual Jun | Actual Jul | Actual Aug | Actual Sep | Oct | Nov | Dec | Actual Jan–Sep Current Year |
|---|---|---|---|---|---|---|---|---|---|---|---|---|---|
| Beginning cash balance | $ 42,880 | $34,025 | $32,975 | $32,445 | $27,476 | $31,139 | $30,926 | $28,196 | $11,672 | | | | $ 42,880 |
| **Section 1** | | | | | | | | | | | | | |
| **Revenues** | | | | | | | | | | | | | |
| Sales | 40,981 | 36,288 | 38,245 | 33,839 | 43,262 | 48,336 | 40,485 | 61,488 | 39,775 | | | | 382,700 |
| Other | 164 | 164 | 164 | 164 | 164 | 164 | 164 | 164 | 164 | | | | 1,476 |
| Total | 41,145 | 36,452 | 38,409 | 34,003 | 43,426 | 48,500 | 40,649 | 61,652 | 39,939 | | | | 384,176 |
| Cost of goods sold | 20,080 | 17,418 | 18,358 | 16,581 | 21,198 | 23,201 | 19,028 | 33,204 | 19,490 | | | | 188,559 |
| Gross profit | 21,065 | 19,034 | 20,051 | 17,422 | 22,228 | 25,299 | 21,621 | 28,448 | 20,449 | | | | 195,617 |
| **Operating expenses** | | | | | | | | | | | | | |
| Employee wages and taxes | 5,316 | 5,176 | 5,023 | 4,832 | 4,836 | 5,424 | 5,324 | 4,865 | 5,039 | | | | 45,835 |
| Rent | 4,684 | 5,269 | 4,684 | 4,684 | 4,684 | 4,684 | 4,684 | 4,684 | 4,684 | | | | 42,743 |
| Advertising and marketing | 1,229 | 1,089 | 1,147 | 1,015 | 1,298 | 1,450 | 1,215 | 1,845 | 1,193 | | | | 11,481 |
| Insurance | 0 | 0 | 0 | 0 | 0 | 0 | 0 | 2,096 | 0 | | | | 2,096 |
| Repairs and maintenance | 0 | 56 | 0 | 0 | 0 | 294 | 0 | 0 | 0 | | | | 350 |
| Telephone and utilities | 925 | 910 | 986 | 932 | 889 | 833 | 917 | 937 | 1,009 | | | | 8,339 |
| Travel, meals, and entertainment | 58 | 27 | 67 | 30 | 136 | 116 | 1,083 | 27 | 0 | | | | 1,543 |
| Credit card and bank fees | 492 | 435 | 459 | 406 | 519 | 580 | 486 | 738 | 477 | | | | 4,592 |
| Legal and accounting | 135 | 135 | 1,255 | 135 | 135 | 135 | 135 | 135 | 135 | | | | 2,335 |
| Office supplies and expenses | 35 | 35 | 35 | 35 | 35 | 35 | 35 | 35 | 35 | | | | 315 |
| Dues and subscriptions | 25 | 25 | 25 | 25 | 25 | 25 | 25 | 25 | 25 | | | | 225 |
| Miscellaneous | 56 | 123 | 109 | 47 | 42 | 58 | 37 | 40 | 36 | | | | 548 |
| Total | 12,956 | 13,280 | 13,791 | 12,141 | 12,599 | 13,635 | 13,940 | 15,426 | 12,634 | | | | 120,402 |
| EBITDA | $ 8,109 | $5,754 | $6,260 | $5,281 | $9,629 | $11,664 | $7,681 | $13,022 | $7,815 | | | | $ 75,215 |

**Section 2**

**Debt service (principal and interest)**

| | | | | | | | | | | Totals |
|---|--:|--:|--:|--:|--:|--:|--:|--:|--:|--:|
| First National Bank | $(1,220) | $(1,220) | $(1,220) | $(1,220) | $(1,220) | $(1,220) | $(1,220) | $(1,220) | $(1,220) | $ (10,979) |
| Other | 0 | 0 | 0 | 0 | 0 | 0 | 0 | 0 | 0 | 0 |
| Totals | (1,220) | (1,220) | (1,220) | (1,220) | (1,220) | (1,220) | (1,220) | (1,220) | (1,220) | (10,979) |

**Section 3**

**Investments**

| | | | | | | | | | | Totals |
|---|--:|--:|--:|--:|--:|--:|--:|--:|--:|--:|
| Capital expenditures | (11,250) | 0 | 0 | 0 | 0 | 0 | 0 | 0 | 0 | (11,250) |
| Other | 0 | 0 | 0 | 0 | 0 | 0 | 0 | 0 | 0 | 0 |
| Totals | (11,250) | 0 | 0 | 0 | 0 | 0 | 0 | 0 | 0 | (11,250) |

**Section 4**

**Other cash flow items and timing differences**

| | | | | | | | | | | Totals |
|---|--:|--:|--:|--:|--:|--:|--:|--:|--:|--:|
| Deduct: sales | (40,981) | (36,288) | (38,245) | (33,839) | (43,262) | (48,336) | (40,485) | (61,488) | (39,775) | (382,700) |
| Add: cash collected from sales and A/R | 40,981 | 36,288 | 37,976 | 34,108 | 43,262 | 48,336 | 40,485 | 43,368 | 39,775 | 364,580 |
| Add: cost of goods sold | 20,081 | 17,418 | 18,358 | 16,581 | 21,198 | 23,201 | 19,028 | 33,203 | 19,490 | 188,559 |
| Deduct: inventory purchases | (16,065) | (17,766) | (18,541) | (16,913) | (20,986) | (29,002) | (18,838) | (43,165) | (35,082) | (216,357) |
| Estimated tax payments | (4,000) | 0 | 0 | (4,000) | 0 | 0 | (4,000) | 0 | 0 | (12,000) |
| Distributions to owner | (5,000) | (5,000) | (5,000) | (5,000) | (5,000) | (5,000) | (5,000) | 0 | 0 | (35,000) |
| Change in accounts payable | 225 | (100) | 50 | (25) | 75 | 100 | (500) | (500) | (500) | (1,175) |
| Other | 265 | (136) | (167) | 57 | (33) | 43 | 119 | 255 | 304 | 707 |
| Totals | (4,494) | (5,584) | (5,569) | (9,031) | (4,746) | (10,657) | (9,191) | (28,326) | (15,788) | (93,386) |
| Net cash flow | (8,855) | (1,050) | (529) | (4,969) | 3,663 | (213) | (2,730) | (16,524) | (9,192) | (40,401) |
| Ending cash balance | $ 34,025 | $ 32,975 | $ 32,445 | $ 27,476 | $ 31,139 | $ 30,926 | $ 28,196 | $ 11,672 | $ 2,480 | |
| Minimum cash balance target | $ 15,000 | $ 15,000 | $ 15,000 | $ 15,000 | $ 15,000 | $ 15,000 | $ 15,000 | $ 15,000 | $ 15,000 | |
| Cash excess (shortfall) | $ 19,025 | $ 17,975 | $ 17,445 | $ 12,476 | $ 16,139 | $ 15,926 | $ 13,196 | $ (3,328) | $(12,520) | |

flow questions—What do I expect my cash balance to be six months from now?

At the point we can answer this question, then we will have the information we need to evaluate the cash flow problems and concerns the owner had expressed when this process started. We will be in a perfect position to see exactly what's going on with the cash flow of the business.

Here is the four-step process for creating accurate projections we discussed in Chapter 12. We followed each of these steps and principles as we created and entered the cash flow projections.

## 1. The Near Future Almost Always Looks a Lot Like the Recent Past

This is a very important principle to look at as you create cash flow projections. Ignoring this principle is why most financial projections are inaccurate and unrealistic. Many business owners have a tendency to let their optimism and confidence in their business run a little wild when they are projecting revenues in this step.

The critical point to remember is that we are projecting the next six months. We are projecting the near future as opposed to the long-term future. An owner may have big plans for the business over time. And those plans could well become reality. However, this step in the process is about projecting the next six months. And the best starting point here is to recognize the reality that the near future almost always looks a lot like the recent past.

We put this principle to work by reviewing the Peace of Mind schedule with the actual results entered. This gave us a perfect view into what the cash flow was likely to be because we had the last nine months of actual cash flow results side-by-side to look at.

The owner was amazed at how helpful it was to see all nine months side-by-side. He saw his financial results and cash flow in a way he had never seen them before. And most importantly, he saw how easy it was to begin creating his cash flow projections with that data right there in front of him.

## 2. Consider What Is Changing

This principle requires that you take a look at whether anything in the business is changing in a significant way such that it would affect your cash flow over the next six months. This is your opportunity to consider whether something may be different in the near future than it was in the recent past.

In our example, the fact that November and December were the two biggest selling months of the year fit the criteria of a significant change. Sales would be much higher in those two months than any of the previous months' sales. We took this fact into account as we estimated what sales would be for those two months.

## 3. Be Conservative

One thing about a projection you can be certain of: it will not be perfectly accurate. In fact, you can be 100 percent certain that the actual results will vary somewhat from what you project.

The trick is to get close—and to err on the side of being conservative.

The sales estimate for November and December provides a good example of how we used this principle in preparing the cash flow projections. We knew that November and December sales would be higher than the previous months' sales because of the holiday selling season.

We looked back at the sales for November and December of the prior year. Sales so far this year were up 14 percent. The first reaction would be to take the sales for those two months and increase them by 14 percent. To be conservative though, we decided to use 5 percent instead. This way, if the sales trend for the year holds up for the last two months of the year, we will have a positive surprise in the cash flow.

Remember, the key is to have a good estimate, but to err on the side of being conservative.

## The 90% Test

Here is a simple test that works wonders. I call it the 90% Test.

We asked ourselves—Are we 90% sure the cash flow projections will come in at or better than we projected? The key here is the phrase "at or better than we projected." If you can answer yes to this question with confidence, then your projections are sufficiently conservative.

We used the 90% Test to make sure we erred on the side of being conservative with our projections.

## 4. Use the "Smell Test"

When the projections were complete, we used this principle to make sure the numbers made sense. The smell test is a quick way I use to make sure everything smells right. It's a way to make sure nothing unusual or unexpected has made its way into the numbers.

We took a good look at each of the four sections of the schedule and the resulting cash balances. We looked to see that the projections were in line with our general expectations. We looked to see that the projections made sense relative to the actual cash flow results portion of the schedule.

This process is a great way to spot errors. We could have accidentally put a decimal in the wrong place, accidentally entered an extra zero, or made some other data entry error. The smell test helps make sure the schedule is error free. The last thing we would want to do to ourselves or the business is to make business decisions based on projected cash balances that are wrong.

Now we have the Peace of Mind schedule set up with actual results for the months of January through September of the current year and projected results for October through March. We have the information we need now to understand what's going on with the cash flow.

Exhibits 5 and 6 show the Peace of Mind schedule as it looked at this stage of the process.

## Key Insights

The next step is to review the schedule and see what it has revealed to us about the business. I like to create a list of "learnings" or "key insights" while I review the completed schedule. This will provide the information to compare to the original list of concerns and worries about the cash flow that lets us see whether we can determine what is causing the cash flow problems. Then we can create the action plan for how we will make the business even better.

We followed the seven-step review process from Chapter 13. Here is a summary of how we went through each of the seven steps and some of the "key insights" we made note of as we reviewed the completed Peace of Mind schedule.

### 1. Understand the Peak and Trough Cash Months

Almost every business will have a month or a portion of the year where their cash balance is generally the highest. They will also have a particular month or period during the year where their cash balance will be at its lowest levels during the year.

It is very important to understand when the peak and the trough periods typically occur and the dollar amount of the difference between the two balances. This helps you plan your financial commitments in a way that ensures your cash flow does not become a problem.

In our example, the peak cash period occurs in the December to February timeframe. This is the time during and just after the busy selling months of November and December. Sales have just been at their highest levels for the year. In addition, a portion of the inventory

# Exhibit 5
## The Home Furnishings Store
## The Peace of Mind Schedule
## Current Year

| | Actual Jan | Actual Feb | Actual Mar | Actual Apr | Actual May | Actual Jun | Actual Jul | Actual Aug | Actual Sep | Projected Oct | Projected Nov | Projected Dec | Projected Current Year |
|---|---|---|---|---|---|---|---|---|---|---|---|---|---|
| Beginning cash balance | $ 42,880 | $ 34,025 | $ 32,975 | $ 32,445 | $ 27,476 | $ 31,139 | $ 30,926 | $ 28,196 | $ 11,672 | $ 2,480 | $ 3,392 | $ 27,844 | $ 42,880 |
| **Section 1** | | | | | | | | | | | | | |
| **Revenues** | | | | | | | | | | | | | |
| Sales | 40,981 | 36,288 | 38,245 | 33,839 | 43,262 | 48,336 | 40,485 | 61,488 | 39,775 | 36,000 | 68,200 | 87,300 | 574,201 |
| Other | 164 | 164 | 164 | 164 | 164 | 164 | 164 | 164 | 164 | 164 | 164 | 164 | 1,968 |
| Total | 41,145 | 36,452 | 38,409 | 34,003 | 43,426 | 48,500 | 40,649 | 61,652 | 39,939 | 36,164 | 68,364 | 87,464 | 576,169 |
| Cost of goods sold | 20,080 | 17,418 | 18,358 | 16,581 | 21,198 | 23,201 | 19,028 | 33,204 | 19,490 | 18,000 | 31,372 | 40,158 | 278,089 |
| Gross profit | 21,065 | 19,034 | 20,051 | 17,422 | 22,228 | 25,299 | 21,621 | 28,448 | 20,449 | 18,164 | 36,992 | 47,306 | 298,080 |
| **Operating expenses** | | | | | | | | | | | | | |
| Employee wages and taxes | 5,316 | 5,176 | 5,023 | 4,832 | 4,836 | 5,424 | 5,324 | 4,865 | 5,039 | 5,200 | 5,600 | 6,200 | 62,835 |
| Rent | 4,684 | 4,684 | 4,684 | 4,684 | 4,684 | 4,684 | 4,684 | 4,684 | 4,684 | 4,684 | 4,684 | 4,684 | 56,795 |
| Advertising and marketing | 1,229 | 1,089 | 1,147 | 1,015 | 1,298 | 1,450 | 1,215 | 1,845 | 1,193 | 1,080 | 2,046 | 2,619 | 17,226 |
| Insurance | 0 | 0 | 0 | 0 | 0 | 0 | 0 | 2,096 | 0 | 0 | 0 | 0 | 2,096 |
| Repairs and maintenance | 0 | 56 | 0 | 0 | 0 | 294 | 0 | 0 | 0 | 50 | 0 | 0 | 400 |
| Telephone and utilities | 925 | 910 | 986 | 932 | 889 | 833 | 917 | 937 | 1,009 | 1,026 | 1,048 | 1,368 | 11,781 |
| Travel, meals, and entertainment | 58 | 27 | 67 | 30 | 136 | 116 | 1,083 | 27 | 0 | 65 | 65 | 65 | 1,738 |
| Credit card and bank fees | 492 | 435 | 459 | 406 | 519 | 580 | 486 | 738 | 477 | 432 | 818 | 1,048 | 6,890 |
| Legal and accounting | 135 | 135 | 135 | 135 | 135 | 135 | 135 | 135 | 135 | 135 | 135 | 135 | 2,740 |
| Office supplies and expenses | 35 | 35 | 35 | 35 | 35 | 35 | 35 | 35 | 35 | 35 | 35 | 35 | 420 |
| Dues and subscriptions | 25 | 25 | 25 | 25 | 25 | 25 | 25 | 25 | 25 | 25 | 75 | 25 | 350 |
| Miscellaneous | 56 | 123 | 109 | 47 | 42 | 58 | 37 | 40 | 36 | 50 | 50 | 50 | 698 |
| Total | 12,956 | 13,280 | 13,791 | 12,141 | 12,599 | 13,635 | 13,940 | 15,426 | 12,634 | 12,782 | 14,557 | 16,229 | 163,970 |
| EBITDA | $ 8,109 | $5,754 | $6,260 | $5,281 | $9,629 | $11,664 | $7,681 | $13,022 | $7,815 | $5,382 | $22,435 | $31,077 | $134,110 |

## Debt service (principal and interest)

| | | | | | | | | | | | | | Totals |
|---|---|---|---|---|---|---|---|---|---|---|---|---|---|
| First National Bank | $(1,220) | $(1,220) | $(1,220) | $(1,220) | $(1,220) | $(1,220) | $(1,220) | $(1,220) | $(1,220) | $(1,220) | $(1,220) | $(1,220) | $(14,639) |
| Other | 0 | 0 | 0 | 0 | 0 | 0 | 0 | 0 | 0 | 0 | 0 | 0 | 0 |
| Totals | (1,220) | (1,220) | (1,220) | (1,220) | (1,220) | (1,220) | (1,220) | (1,220) | (1,220) | (1,220) | (1,220) | (1,220) | (14,639) |

## Section 3

### Investments

| | | | | | | | | | | | | | Totals |
|---|---|---|---|---|---|---|---|---|---|---|---|---|---|
| Capital expenditures | (11,250) | 0 | 0 | 0 | 0 | 0 | 0 | 0 | (250) | 0 | 0 | 0 | (11,500) |
| Other | 0 | 0 | 0 | 0 | 0 | 0 | 0 | 0 | 0 | 0 | 0 | 0 | 0 |
| Totals | (11,250) | 0 | 0 | 0 | 0 | 0 | 0 | 0 | (250) | 0 | 0 | 0 | (11,500) |

## Section 4

### Other cash flow items and timing differences

| | | | | | | | | | | | | | Totals |
|---|---|---|---|---|---|---|---|---|---|---|---|---|---|
| Deduct: sales | (40,981) | (36,288) | (38,245) | (33,839) | (43,262) | (48,336) | (40,485) | (61,488) | (39,775) | (36,000) | (68,200) | (87,300) | (574,201) |
| Add: cash collected from sales and A/R | 40,981 | 36,288 | 37,976 | 34,108 | 43,262 | 48,336 | 40,485 | 43,368 | 39,775 | 43,800 | 78,400 | 87,300 | 574,081 |
| Add: cost of goods sold | 20,081 | 17,418 | 18,358 | 16,581 | 21,198 | 23,201 | 19,028 | 33,203 | 19,490 | 18,000 | 31,372 | 40,158 | 278,089 |
| Deduct: inventory purchases | (16,065) | (17,766) | (18,541) | (16,913) | (20,986) | (29,002) | (18,838) | (43,165) | (35,082) | (25,200) | (28,235) | (22,087) | (291,879) |
| Estimated tax payments | (4,000) | 0 | 0 | (4,000) | 0 | 0 | (4,000) | 0 | 0 | (4,000) | 0 | 0 | (16,000) |
| Distributions to owner | (5,000) | (5,000) | (5,000) | (5,000) | (5,000) | (5,000) | (5,000) | 0 | 0 | (10,000) | 0 | (15,000) | (60,000) |
| Change in accounts payable | 225 | (100) | 50 | (25) | 75 | 100 | (500) | (500) | (500) | 100 | 100 | 100 | (875) |
| Other | 265 | (136) | (167) | 57 | (33) | 43 | 119 | 255 | 304 | 50 | 50 | 50 | 857 |
| Totals | (4,494) | (5,584) | (5,569) | (9,031) | (4,746) | (10,657) | (9,191) | (28,326) | (15,788) | (13,250) | 13,487 | 3,221 | (89,928) |
| Net cash flow | (8,855) | (1,050) | (529) | (4,969) | 3,663 | (213) | (2,730) | (16,524) | (9,192) | 912 | 24,452 | 33,079 | 18,043 |
| Ending cash balance | $34,025 | $32,975 | $32,445 | $27,476 | $31,139 | $30,926 | $28,196 | $11,672 | $2,480 | $3,392 | $27,844 | $60,923 | $60,923 |
| Minimum cash balance target | $15,000 | $15,000 | $15,000 | $15,000 | $15,000 | $15,000 | $15,000 | $15,000 | $15,000 | $15,000 | $15,000 | $15,000 | $15,000 |
| Cash excess (shortfall) | $19,025 | $17,975 | $17,445 | $12,476 | $16,139 | $15,926 | $13,196 | $(3,328) | $(12,520) | $(11,608) | $12,844 | $45,923 | $45,923 |

# Exhibit 6

## The Home Furnishings Store
## The Peace of Mind Schedule
## Next Year

| | Projected Jan | Projected Feb | Projected Mar | Apr | May | Jun | Jul | Aug | Sep | Oct | Nov | Dec | Projected Jan–Mar Next Year |
|---|---|---|---|---|---|---|---|---|---|---|---|---|---|
| Beginning cash balance | $ 60,923 | $ 63,400 | $ 63,332 | | | | | | | | | | $ 60,923 |
| **Section 1** | | | | | | | | | | | | | |
| **Revenues** | | | | | | | | | | | | | |
| Sales | 43,000 | 38,100 | 40,200 | | | | | | | | | | 121,300 |
| Other | 164 | 164 | 164 | | | | | | | | | | 492 |
| Total | 43,164 | 38,264 | 40,364 | | | | | | | | | | 121,792 |
| Cost of goods sold | 21,070 | 18,288 | 19,296 | | | | | | | | | | 58,654 |
| Gross profit | 22,094 | 19,976 | 21,068 | | | | | | | | | | 63,138 |
| **Operating expenses** | | | | | | | | | | | | | |
| Employee wages and taxes | 5,450 | 5,300 | 5,200 | | | | | | | | | | 15,950 |
| Rent | 4,667 | 5,368 | 4,667 | | | | | | | | | | 14,701 |
| Advertising and marketing | 1,290 | 1,143 | 1,206 | | | | | | | | | | 3,639 |
| Insurance | 0 | 0 | 0 | | | | | | | | | | 0 |
| Repairs and maintenance | 47 | 50 | 0 | | | | | | | | | | 97 |
| Telephone and utilities | 900 | 900 | 900 | | | | | | | | | | 2,700 |
| Travel, meals, and entertainment | 55 | 55 | 55 | | | | | | | | | | 165 |
| Credit card and bank fees | 516 | 457 | 482 | | | | | | | | | | 1,456 |
| Legal and accounting | 126 | 126 | 1,230 | | | | | | | | | | 1,482 |
| Office supplies and expenses | 35 | 35 | 35 | | | | | | | | | | 105 |
| Dues and subscriptions | 25 | 25 | 25 | | | | | | | | | | 75 |
| Miscellaneous | 150 | 150 | 150 | | | | | | | | | | 450 |
| Total | 13,261 | 13,609 | 13,950 | | | | | | | | | | 40,820 |
| EBITDA | $ 8,833 | $ 6,367 | $ 7,118 | | | | | | | | | | $ 22,318 |

## Section 2
### Debt service (principal and interest)

|  |  |  |  |  |
|---|---|---|---|---|
| First National Bank | $ (1,220) | $ (1,220) | $ (1,220) | $ (3,660) |
| Other | 0 | 0 | 0 | 0 |
| Totals | (1,220) | (1,220) | (1,220) | (3,660) |

## Section 3
### Investments

|  |  |  |  |  |
|---|---|---|---|---|
| Capital expenditures | 0 | 0 | 0 | 0 |
| Other | 0 | 0 | 0 | 0 |
| Totals | 0 | 0 | 0 | 0 |

## Section 4
### Other cash flow items and timing differences

|  |  |  |  |  |
|---|---|---|---|---|
| Deduct: sales | (43,000) | (38,100) | (40,200) | (121,300) |
| Add: cash collected from sales and A/R | 43,000 | 38,100 | 40,200 | 121,300 |
| Add: cost of goods sold | 21,070 | 18,288 | 19,296 | 58,654 |
| Deduct: inventory purchases | (16,856) | (18,654) | (20,454) | (55,964) |
| Estimated tax payments | (4,500) | 0 | 0 | (4,500) |
| Distributions to owner | (5,000) | (5,000) | (5,000) | (15,000) |
| Change in accounts payable | 100 | 100 | 100 | 300 |
| Other | 50 | 50 | 50 | 150 |
| Totals | (5,136) | (5,216) | (6,008) | (16,360) |
| Net cash flow | 2,477 | (69) | (110) | 2,299 |
| Ending cash balance | $ 63,400 | $ 63,332 | $ 63,222 | $ 63,222 |
| Minimum cash balance target | $ 15,000 | $ 15,000 | $ 15,000 | $ 15,000 |
| Cash excess (shortfall) | $ 48,400 | $ 48,332 | $ 48,222 | $ 48,222 |

he is selling does not need to be replaced right away. Some of the inventory was intentionally built up during the summer months so it was available to sell during the peak selling period. Therefore inventory levels can be maintained at lower levels after December and inventory purchases reduced. We will look more at inventory in step #5 below.

The trough cash period occurs in the September to October period. This is the time when inventory is being ordered and paid for in order to have the store properly stocked for November and December. In Exhibit 5 you will see that his cash balance at the end of September of the current year was just under $2,500 (well below the minimum cash target of $15,000).

His projected cash balance at the end of October of the current year was not much higher. In fact, he could not make his normal $5,000 distribution to himself beginning in August because he had to protect his cash balance. He planned to begin making the distribution again in November once he got through the trough month.

One of the first insights he had as he looked at the trough period was how that created one of the only consistent complaints he heard from his customers. During November and December he would frequently hear from customers who were frustrated because he had sold out of certain key products. Some of the customers were willing to wait the 45 to 60 days it took to order and receive the product. However, most of the customers were either unwilling or unable to wait that long. He knew he was losing thousands of dollars of sales because he was out of stock on those items.

As he looked back on it, he could see clearly why this problem was happening. He could remember holding back on some of his inventory purchases during those months because he was already worried about how to get all his invoices paid. He felt like the only prudent thing to do was to hold off on some of the orders so he could avoid making his cash flow problem even worse. He had to make these very important inventory buying decisions at the very time he was in his trough cash flow period.

That sinking feeling and anxiety that he felt in October was causing him to make the wrong buying decisions. Fear became the driver of his business decisions rather than the facts. He was confident that a change in how he planned his inventory purchases during that critical period would have a dramatic effect on revenues during the critical selling season. He made a note on his key insights list that he would handle this differently next year.

### 2. Review Your Debt Service Obligations

His debt service obligations were very straightforward. He made a payment each month on his note with the bank. The note still had several more years to go before it was paid off. There were no balloon payments scheduled so there were no unusual or one-time payments to consider.

At this point, he had no immediate plans to borrow any additional money. He still had a desire to open another location sometime, but he was determined to make sure he had the cash flow of his current location performing properly before he opened another store.

### 3. Pay Special Attention to Capital Expenditures

His only major capital expenditure was the purchase of a delivery van in January of the current year. He bought the van with cash since he had a nice cash balance at the time. One of the insights he had here was to make sure a large purchase like that in the future was made based on what impact it would have on the trough month rather than just whether he had the cash at the time of the purchase.

### 4. A Sale Is Not Complete Until the Cash Is Collected

We looked at each month in the current year to see the relationship between the store's sales and the cash collected. The store makes virtually all its sales in cash, check, or credit card. This means almost all their sales are collected at the time the customer makes the purchase in the store. You would then expect the sales and the cash collected lines to be pretty much the same each month.

The two lines were pretty much the same until the month of August. If you look at the schedule in Exhibit 5, you will see that sales in August of the current year were $61,488 but cash collected during that month was only $43,368. There was a difference of just over $18,000 between the two amounts. And this difference was not collected in September either.

This meant the income statement included just over $18,000 of sales that had never made it to the owner's cash balance—they had never been collected. The bookkeeper had the answer for us very quickly when we asked about the difference. It turns out the owner had been focusing on developing relationships with businesses and organizations that make large purchases for their offices or other facilities. This was a market he had never really tapped into before.

In August he sold about $18,000 of merchandise to two different accounts. He had basically hit a home run by winning these two new commercial accounts. He was feeling really good about the sales and about finally breaking into this untapped market. And his income statement looked really good in the month he made the sales. In fact, it showed he had the best August in the store's history.

What he had not realized until now was that these sales were actually hurting his cash flow. Not only had he never collected the $18,000, he had already paid for the inventory he sold them. The merchandise was specially ordered for these customers and paid for in June.

This uncollected sale was happening at a time of the year when he could least afford to be without the cash. The sale looked good in the income statement, but not so good in the Peace of Mind schedule.

## 5. Inventory Can Hurt You Real Fast

We reviewed the two lines in section 4 that pertain to inventory—cost of goods sold and inventory purchases. Take a minute to look at these two lines in Exhibit 5.

You can see that inventory purchases are less than cost of goods sold in January, are pretty much the same as cost of goods sold for February through May, then go up significantly relative to cost of goods sold for June through September. This increase in purchases during the summer months is part of the cycle where inventory is being bought in order to be ready for the seasonally stronger fourth quarter.

One thing that was unusual this year was the spike in purchases in June. The reason purchases went up so much that early in the summer was the commercial sale we discussed above. The inventory that he sold to the commercial accounts was paid for in June.

Inventory purchases were projected to be significantly less than cost of goods sold for November and December. The reason for that reduction is he is selling inventory during the strong selling season that does not need to be replaced. This has the effect of bringing the inventory levels back down a bit since inventory does not need to be as high once the key selling season is over.

## 6. Paying Your Taxes Requires Good Planning (and Thinking Inside the Box)

Our business owner did a very good job of working closely with the bookkeeper and his CPA to plan his estimated tax payments. He made payments quarterly based on the taxes he estimated to be due once the year was over.

He met with his CPA once a quarter to review his financial results for the quarter that just passed and to look at his projections for the rest of the year. From here they decided whether to change his estimated taxes. They also used that time to consider and implement tax saving ideas.

They did their tax planning in a very prudent way. They recognized that pushing the envelope of the tax laws is not an effective business strategy. They made sure they took every deduction possible while making sure they "colored inside the lines."

## 7. Watch Accounts Payable Closely

The change in accounts payable never varied greatly during the year. As a result, there was nothing he needed to do to improve in this area except to continue to watch the accounts payable closely and make sure he was getting his vendors paid on or before the due date.

## Put the Key Insights into Action

Now it was time to take the insights and learning from our in-depth review of the Peace of Mind schedule and put his "next steps" in writing. This is the part of the process where we create the action plan for how we will improve the business and its cash flow.

- He decided to always have a good view into the peak and trough cash months. To do this, he committed to always have at least twelve months of cash flow projections in the Peace of Mind schedule. This would help him make sure he could see exactly how every financial decision he was considering would affect his trough month cash balance. Whether the financial decision was being made in January or October, the decision would still be made based on what the expected impact would be on the September to October cash balance. This decision alone will relieve a huge amount of the worry and concern he felt in the past.

- He learned a very important lesson about selling to commercial accounts. He learned that selling something and collecting the money can be two different things. He created new standards for how these sales would be handled in the future.

Each invoice for a commercial sale would have a specific due date on it. He began talking to his commercial customers about his terms very early in the selling process. Having this worked into the selling process early on helped him make sure his invoice would get processed in a timely fashion once it was sent to the company. He also decided to begin a proactive process for calling to check the status of an invoice within seven days of sending it. He would have his bookkeeper make frequent calls to check the status of any outstanding invoices so he could aggressively work outstanding invoices before they could become a problem.

He also planned to make sure he understood the full cash flow impact of accepting large orders. He now recognized that it is very important to know that you have sufficient cash flow to handle the up-front cash commitment required to take on a big new order from a customer.

- He planned to create a new initiative that would help relieve the pressure on his cash flow being created by the inventory buying cycle. The plan was to work with his merchandise vendors to get better terms for the payment of their invoices. If he could get special "dating" on orders placed in August and September, then he could significantly improve his trough cash balance.

Special invoice dating would mean that invoices from the vendor created during that two-month period would have a due date at the end of December rather than the normal 30-day terms. This would move the due date for those invoices into a month where his cash balance is much stronger. It would move the due date out of the trough period and into the peak cash balance period. This would totally alleviate the intense cash flow pressure he felt when so many invoices had to be paid.

In order to make this proposal attractive for his vendors, he was prepared to show them how they could sell even more product to him than they were selling now. He let them know that he would begin shifting more of his purchases to the vendor that would provide him the December dating he was looking for. He currently did business with a number of vendors. He was prepared to reduce the number of vendors and therefore move more of his buying to the vendors that helped him achieve his objectives.

He also would help them see how the new invoice terms would allow him to solve an important customer complaint while at the same time helping the vendors. The new invoice terms would help him make sure he was better stocked going into the busy selling season. He would be able to buy more product and make sure he never ran out of the top selling merchandise. This would mean less out of stock problems with customers, more business for the vendors, and more sales for him. This would create a true win-win-win for everyone.

- He committed to have the Peace of Mind schedule updated every month so he always knew exactly what was going on with the cash flow of his business. He recognized that his time was better spent managing the store and making sure he was doing everything possible to bring in new customers and keep existing customers happy. He would not be the person updating the schedule each month, but he would make sure it was done each month. He would always have the benefit of having the cash flow of the store in front of him as he made important business decisions.

This exercise proved to be a very valuable one for our business owner. He finally saw what was really going on with the cash flow of his business. He saw for the first time a presentation of his cash flow in a way that made perfect sense. It was not clouded and hidden within his financial statements. It was presented clearly and logically in a way that made what was going on crystal clear.

I have seen it happen over and over again where once owners see a clear and logical presentation of their cash flow they almost instantly see solutions to their pressing problems and concerns. They can quickly set out what they need to do to fix the problem. And the most interesting part of all is that the fix is almost always a result of taking very few actions. Just a few things done differently can eliminate the problems and concerns that were nagging and eating at them just a few days before.

In our example, working with the vendors for a fairly small invoice due date concession during September and October fixes the majority of the problems he identified. The core problem was producing a number of undesirable effects. A new approach to proactively and consciously managing his trough cash month made all the difference.

He felt a huge sense of relief. He could now reclaim all the lost time and wasted effort that previously went into worrying about his cash flow and fighting the cash flow fire with vendors every year. He could now use all his time working more closely with customers and working more closely with his merchandise vendors to get the best selling merchandise into the store. They could work together to make sure he was always in stock on the hot selling product. He could also focus more on the all-important task of constantly getting and keeping customers.

## Your Action Plan

✔ Use the example business in this chapter as your guide for taking control of your cash flow. All it requires is your decision to either do the work yourself or have someone else do it for you.

✔ Answering the two critical cash flow questions is the key to your financial success. Everything you need to properly manage your cash flow comes from answering these two simple questions.

✔ A relatively small number of problems (the core problems) create the majority of the frustrations, complications, and concerns (the undesirable effects) that fill a businessperson's mind each day. Find the core problems that have been keeping you from creating the business you have always dreamed of.

✔ Remember, it's not what you say you are going to do that counts—it's what you actually do. Commit to persist until you succeed.

## Send Me Your Questions

If you have any questions, concerns, or comments, please feel free to send them to me at pcampbell@growandsucceed.com. I respond to all my e-mail personally and promptly.

# PART FOUR

## Your Willingness to Use a Proven Solution

# Chapter 16

## The Most Common Cash Flow "Yes, buts . . ."

*Many of life's failures are people who did not realize how close they were to success when they gave up.*
—THOMAS EDISON, INVENTOR

A "Yes, but" happens when you say, "Yes, that's a great idea. I agree I need to do that, but . . . what about . . . and what about . . . ?"

Basically, you agree with what needs to be done, but something is preventing you from actually doing it. You have a thought or concern that is keeping you from taking action right now.

A "Yes, but" is a natural result of thinking through the implications of trying something new. It is healthy to look at advice from someone and consider possible obstacles as to why it may not work.

There are always obstacles between you and what you desire or what you want to accomplish. It is good planning to consider those obstacles. The key though is not only to identify the obstacles, but also to take action to get them out of your way.

This chapter will help you do just that. It will help you toss aside the obstacles that have prevented you from taking control of your cash flow the way you know you really should.

163

I have identified some of the most common "Yes, buts" that I have heard over the years. Look at each one to see if any of these doubts are holding you back from taking control of your cash flow. If one or more of them is holding you back, give some serious thought to whether your fear or concern is really valid.

Stop and ask yourself this question: Is my business really better off the way I am doing it now? Or would the tips and strategies I have learned in this book serve my business and me better?

Use these "Yes, buts" to test your own thinking and to help you put these principles to work today. Each one relates to a possible obstacle and what you need to do to remove it from your path.

**Yes, but . . . :** I don't have time to take care of the books.

**Answer:** Cash Flow Rule #5 says either you do the work or have someone else do it. If you don't have the time to make sure you have an accurate cash balance, then you really have no other choice but to have someone else do it.

If you make the decision (either consciously or by just letting it happen) that nobody will be responsible for maintaining an accurate cash balance, then you are setting yourself up to fail. It's obvious that a business that does not know what's going on with the cash balance will eventually spin out of control and fail.

It's like finding a small leak in your roof and not doing anything about it. Over time it will only get bigger. The problem will not fix itself. It will only get worse and cause even more damage. Either you fix it or you have someone else fix it. That way you avoid the more serious and long-term implications of neglecting the leak. You need to have it fixed now while it is still small and easy to repair.

The same approach works with taking control of your cash flow. All you need to do to fix the problem is decide who you will have do the work. That's not difficult. Just make the decision and the issue goes away.

If you are not sure who to ask to do the work, talk to your CPA or accountant. They are in an excellent position to help you get this work done.

**Yes, but . . . :** I have to be out with customers and prospects, not behind a desk or in front of the computer.

**Answer:** There is a saying that goes like this: Nothing happens until someone sells something. That's a very true statement. In most small businesses, the owner is also the main salesperson. The owner is oftentimes the primary person out there creating revenues for the business.

Therefore, I definitely agree that you have to be driving the revenue line in a big way.

Your mission is to help customers part with their money, pure and simple. And you want to do it in a way that the customers are delighted with you and they refer many new customers to you. That's the kind of business that produces a lot of cash.

You may be getting hung up on this "Yes, but . . ." because part of it says "not behind a desk or in front of the computer." It makes several assumptions that are not necessarily true.

First, it assumes you will be doing the work.

This may be true or may not be true. Remember Cash Flow Rule #5: Either you do the work or have someone else do it. If you are the person doing the work to make sure you can answer the two critical cash flow questions, you should look at that decision to see if you need to change it.

If you have come to the conclusion that you are hurting the business when you do that work, then it's time to have someone else do it so you can spend more of your time with your prospects and customers. You will actually save money and become even more effective.

**Yes, but . . . :** I've always handled my finances the same way; I'm not sure I can change now.

**Answer:** Sure you can, but it requires some work on your part. You need to both think differently and manage the cash flow of your business differently.

We all tend to be creatures of habit rather than creatures of logic. As a result, breaking old habits can be tough. It's even difficult sometimes to break a habit we know is not serving our values or helping us get what we want.

The good news with your cash flow is that you have exactly what you need now to make the change. The process is easy and does not take a long time to implement.

*Never Run Out of Cash* was created as a step-by-step guide to help you get your cash flow under control. It shows you how to eliminate your cash flow worries. Make the commitment now to put it to work for you. It will transform the way you manage your business. You will never go back to the old ways again.

**Yes, but . . . :** How can I predict the future? My business is unpredictable; I can't know what is going to happen six months from now.

**Answer:** It's true you don't know exactly what will happen over the next six months. However, you should have a good idea of what you *expect* to happen.

Unless you just started your business, you have a history. You have a history of actual revenues and actual expenses. You have a cost structure in place and an idea of what you expect to achieve each month. Having a history of results helps make the projection process much easier.

You should also have a good idea of what you want to happen, how you are going to make it happen, and the likelihood of your success. Between your goals and plans for the business and your actual results, you have a sound basis for making reasonable projections.

Think a minute about the worst case scenario with respect to making projections. What if you create the Peace of Mind Schedule and the numbers turn out to be way off from what actually happens? What do you do then?

The answer is you make a new projection. This time, though, you will have learned something about the business and the cash flow projection process. I think that after you do this a few times, you will find your projections become increasingly accurate. It's really quite easy after you get started with it. The Peace of Mind Schedule will become a tool that you will never try to run your business without.

**Yes, but . . . :** I get financial statements each month. Isn't that all I need in order to manage the financial aspects of my business?

**Answer:** The resounding reply to this question is NO.

The basic financial statements you review and analyze each month are useful; in fact, they are a must. You couldn't run a business properly without them.

The income statement, the balance sheet, and the cash flow statement are the traditional financial statements used to show the financial results of any business. Banks require that you provide them. Investors require you to provide them. They are the common language of business.

The problem is that the financial statements are always historical, meaning they are focused on presenting you with what happened in the past. This is critical financial information. However, you must also have a tool for projecting your cash flows into the future.

You have to know what your financial results were in prior months, what your balances are right now, and what you expect the cash balance to be over at least the next six months.

The basic financial statements take care of the first two requirements. The Peace of Mind Schedule will take care of the third requirement.

Another reason the basic financial statements alone are not sufficient is because of the cash flow statement. Its name suggests that it would be the perfect tool to use to manage your cash flow.

**It's not!**

The basic problem with the cash flow statement is the format and approach used to create it. It basically works backward from net income in an attempt to give the reader an idea of the basic changes in the cash balance for the period being presented.

Don't try to use it as a tool for managing your cash flow. That's not what it was designed to do.

To properly manage your cash flow each month, use the Peace of Mind Schedule. It's the right tool for answering the question, what do I expect my cash balance to be six months from now?

## COMMON "UNSPOKEN" ROADBLOCKS

We have discussed some of the most common questions I hear from business owners about how to take control of their cash flow. I addressed each one and how to remove each "Yes, but" from your path.

Now I would like to go over several additional obstacles that get in the way of business owners. These are obstacles that I have observed over the years as I have helped owners implement the cash flow principles. What is interesting here is that I began to notice certain issues that were the "questions behind the questions."

Owners were not specifically verbalizing these concerns, but I could see the concern they had that they were not actually telling me about.

Look at each of these roadblocks to see if they apply to you. If they do, pay close attention to the tips and strategies about how to eliminate these barriers to your success.

- **They Were Scared of What the Cash Flow Projection Might Show.** Many people realize intuitively that the cash flow, or the cash balance, isn't going to be what they want it to be. They're scared of knowing the truth.

  That's operating out of a sense of fear. While we're all prone to fearful thoughts on occasion, we should also recognize that this kind of thinking seldom leads to anything good or productive.

When you close your eyes to what's coming, you are giving away your power. You're giving away your control. You need to have a good sense for where the cash balance is expected to be because it's the lifeblood of the business. You're in business to achieve a certain level of cash, wealth, or success.

And even if the financial aspects are secondary for you, if the cash ever runs out, all those things disappear.

Therefore, if you sense that you aren't doing the work out of a sense of fear from what you may learn, you have to make a commitment to yourself to work through it. Just do it. That's how you regain power over your business and your cash flow.

- **I'm Afraid It Will Cost Too Much.** Many business owners are afraid it will cost too much to have someone do this work for them. My answer to that concern is that the Peace of Mind Schedule is quite easy to create and maintain.

  If you present the schedule and instructions to your accountant or CPA, they can do the work at a reasonable cost. Try it and see. In either case, the work has to be done.

  It's like mowing the lawn. What would happen if you didn't mow the lawn and you didn't have someone else do it for you? The grass would keep on growing. The weeds would keep on multiplying.

  You would quickly have a yard that was an embarrassment to you, your family, and your neighbors. Yes, you will have saved some time and maybe saved some money—at least temporarily. The problem is the lawn still has to be mowed. The weeds still have to be pulled. All you would have done would be to make the work even harder for yourself or more expensive when you pay someone to do it for you.

169

It's the same with the work necessary to take control of your cash flow. Stop and ask yourself this question: Am I taking better care of my lawn than I am my cash flow? Now that's an interesting (and revealing) question!

Make sure you can answer it the way you know you should. Otherwise it will cost you much, much more to try to do it later.

# Your Action Plan

✔ There are always obstacles (real or perceived) between you and what you want to accomplish. Use the tips and strategies in this chapter to break through those obstacles.

✔ Taking control of your cash flow is not a luxury. It is the key to your financial success in business. Commit to doing what it takes to take control—**now.**

✔ Look back at each of the "Yes, buts" in this chapter to see if any of them ring true for you. Then, follow the advice provided for each one so that you can get past the obstacle.

# Send Me Your Questions

If you have any questions, concerns, or comments, please feel free to send them to me at pcampbell@growandsucceed.com. I respond to all my e-mail personally and promptly.

# Chapter 17

## Taking Control of
## Your Cash Flow

*We are what we repeatedly do. Excellence,*
*then, is not an act, but a habit.*
—ARISTOTLE, PHILOSOPHER

Congratulations for hanging in there with me to the end. That kind of commitment tells me (and should also tell you) that you are prepared to do what it takes to regain control of your cash flow.

It will take some work to get started. Anything new takes a little investment of time and effort. Then, as you get into the process, you will begin to see exciting results.

You will begin to experience the peace of mind that comes from having your cash flow under control. You will have a newfound understanding of the lifeblood of your business—your CASH.

No more wondering what's going on. No more feeling helpless as you consider the important business decisions that must be made every day.

Now you know you did the right thing by implementing the step-by-step process you learned in this book. You are on the right path! Running your business is becoming *fun* again.

# WHAT I DO VERSUS WHAT I MUST DO

The Greek philosopher Aristotle said that our habits have a tremendous impact on what we accomplish. In many respects, they define who we are. He said:

> "We are what we repeatedly do. Excellence, then, is not an act, but a habit."
>
> —*Aristotle*

Your job in putting these cash flow principles to work is to make them a habit. Make the step-by-step process in this book a habit. Make them as much a part of you as brushing your teeth. (Now you see why I had you put a copy of The 10 Cash Flow Rules up on your mirror!) It will transform the way you manage your business.

Take time now to complete these short exercises. They will help you to clarify exactly what you need to do in order to regain control over your cash flow and your business.

**Exercise #1**

These are the habits I *currently practice* during a typical week to make sure I have the cash flow of my business under control:

1._____

_____

2._____

_____

3._____

_____

4._____

_____

5._____

_____

6._____

_____

7._____

_____

8._____

_____

9._____

_____

10._____

_____

## Exercise #2

These are the habits that I know, deep down, if I practiced in a consistent way, would enormously increase my level of success and would also greatly decrease my chance of failure:

1._____

_____

2._____

_____

3._____

_____

4._____

_____

5._____

_____

6._____

_____

7._____

_____

8._____

_____

9._____

_____

10._____

_____

## Your Action Plan

✔ Look back at Chapter 2, How You Can Benefit from Getting Your Cash Flow Under Control. Review the benefits that are yours for the taking. These can be yours by putting the cash flow principles in this book to work in your business.

✔ The choices you make and the habits you possess say a great deal about what is important to you. Choose to form the cash flow habits that successful business owners possess. Do it **NOW.**

✔ In the section of this chapter titled What I Do Versus What I Must Do, complete Exercises 1 and 2. These short exercises will get you started on the road to a bright new future for your business.

## Send Me Your Questions

If you have any questions, concerns, or comments, please feel free to send them to me at pcampbell@growandsucceed.com. I respond to all my e-mail personally and promptly.

# Help Is Available

I wrote *Never Run Out of Cash* out of a strong desire to help you eliminate your cash flow worries and to help you make your business a financial success. By learning how to take control of the cash flow of your business, it is inevitable that your cash flow worries will begin to disappear and the likelihood of your success will increase.

There are a number of ways you can get help to implement your new approach to managing your cash flow. You can learn and do it yourself. You can have your CPA or accountant do it. You can also have someone in your organization or even a friend who is numbers-oriented do it for you.

If you would like me to implement this process for you, feel free to send me an e-mail and let me know. You can also visit my web site at www.neverrunoutofcash.com/freetools.htm to learn more about how I can help you take control of your cash flow.

My e-mail address is pcampbell@growandsucceed.com. You can call me at 713-962-1646 or send me a fax at 713-559-8356.

# Your Feedback Is Extremely Valuable

I would enjoy hearing about your success in putting the principles in this book to work in your business. Please take time now to send me a note about the parts of the book that really helped you.

Were there any particular chapters that especially spoke to you? Were there chapters that helped you see exactly what you need to do or that were particularly motivating for you?

On the other hand, were there chapters that were vague or unclear to you? Were there parts of the book you felt uncomfortable with or you thought were unclear?

Please let me know what you think. Your feedback will make the book even more helpful when the next edition is released.

Remember, Cash Is King—because No Cash = No Business.

Philip Campbell
pcampbell@growandsucceed.com

# Resources to Help You

I am always providing new tips, strategies, and tools (many of which are FREE) at www.neverrunoutofcash.com/freetools.htm. You will want to check here often so you don't miss out on the new material.

I will also be posting FREE articles and e-courses to the web site as they become available.

*Check it out* NOW and see what's new.

## RECOMMENDED RESOURCE LIST

Over the years, I have amassed a library of more than 400 books and approximately 50 audio learning programs. I have always loved to learn as much as possible about business and how to succeed.

Business owners often ask me to recommend some of the best books and programs to them. This way they get the benefit of the best information available without the trouble of buying and reading hundreds of books and programs.

I have posted a list on my web site in response to those requests. If a particular book or program intrigues you, then go for it. The magical formula for getting what you want in business (and in life) works like this:

1. **Learn** from those who are already successful.
2. **Grow** your ability to make a difference. Grow your ability to make things happen. Grow your mind.
3. **Succeed** at getting what you want. Achieve your dreams and desires.

Take the first step in the process by committing to learn more about being successful in business.

An investment in learning is oftentimes one of the best investments you will ever make. It's the gift to yourself that keeps on giving year after year.

It's also a wonderful gift for your friends and associates who want to be successful in business.

I have put the list on my web site so you can get the most up-to-date resources to help you transform the way you manage your business. I keep this list current.

Go to www.neverrunoutofcash.com/freetools.htm and click on the link to the recommended resources.

Feel free to contact me if you have any questions or if you need help achieving your goals.

Philip Campbell
Phone: 713-962-1646
Fax: 713-559-8356
pcampbell@growandsucceed.com

# Become a Hero to Your Customers

*Never Run Out of Cash* is available at quantity discounts for you to use as a special gift for your valued customers, a premium you can use in sales promotions, or any other creative revenue-generating purposes you may have for your business.

Just think about how you will benefit from providing a valuable gift to your customers:

- Your customers will appreciate your gift. Your name will be on their minds because none of your competition has taken the time to send them a special gift.
- They will appreciate your providing them with a book that can help them take control of their business . . . and their cash flow.
- They will view you more favorably than your competition.

*Never Run Out of Cash* is the perfect gift for anyone who owns or manages a business.

The title and subject will grab their attention. Your gift or promotional piece will stand out even more in their mind when it goes to them with *Never Run Out of Cash* as a gift.

You will position yourself perfectly with your prospect or customer. You will be giving them another reason to do business with you rather than your competition.

Try it. It could be just the idea you need to call attention to your business and grow your revenues . . . and your cash balance.

Please complete the order form at the end of the book and we will help you become a hero to your customers. If you have any questions please call 713-962-1646 or e-mail me at pcampbell@ growandsucceed.com, or visit www.neverrunoutofcash.com/freetools. htm.

Philip Campbell
22211 Buescher Rd.
Tomball, TX 77377
713-962-1646
pcampbell@growandsucceed.com

# The *Cash Is King* Newsletter

If you have not already subscribed to the *Cash Is King* newsletter, do it now. The newsletter is delivered to your e-mail inbox every month. And best of all—It's FREE. It is packed with new tips and strategies to help you take control of your cash. The newsletter brings you loads of valuable advice and guidance to keep you focused on your most precious asset—your cash.

Subscribe now at www.neverrunoutofcash.com/freetools.htm. It's FREE.

# About the Author

Philip Campbell began his business career in 1983 in public accounting. He became a CPA in 1986. Philip spent over six years working with both small and large clients in the areas of accounting, auditing, financial statement preparation and analysis, as well as federal and state income tax consultation and tax return preparation.

After leaving the public accounting field, Philip served in officer level financial positions and has been a member of the management team of each of the companies he has been a part of.

What really sets Philip apart from the average financial person you meet is his passion and excitement about helping business owners take control of their cash flow. Early on in his business career he focused on and "preached" so much about the importance of cash flow that people now call him **CASH.**

Philip is one of those rare individuals who is skilled in the numbers side of business, but who also understands and loves all the different aspects of growing a successful business.

Philip has helped hundreds of business owners take control of their cash flow.

You can contact Philip by e-mail at pcampbell@growandsucceed. com or by phone at 713-962-1646. You can also learn more about Philip and the services he provides at www.neverrunoutofcash.com.

# Order Form

Name: _____

Mailing Address: _____

_____

City & State: _____

Zip Code: _____

Telephone: _____

Fax: _____

E-mail: _____

Please send _____ copy (copies) of *Never Run Out of Cash* @ $16.95 per copy.

Please bill my credit card.

Credit card:    Visa ❑        MC ❑        Amex ❑

Card No: _____

Exp date: _____

Signature of cardholder: _____

Code: _____

Please mail your order form to:

BookMasters, Inc.
30 Amberwood Parkway
Ashland, OH 44805
800-247-6553

You may fax your order to: 419-281-6883

E-mail your order to: order@bookmasters.com

Order through our web site: http://www.atlasbooks.com